DICTATORSHIP AND REVOLUTION

DICTATORSHIP AND REVOLUTION

Iran - A Contemporary History

STRUAN STEVENSON

Dictatorship and Revolution

First published in February 2023

The International Committee in Search of Justice (ISJ)

ISBN-10: 94-6475-224-6 (Hardcover)

ISBN- 978-94-6475-224-3 (Hardcover)

ISBN-10: 94-6475-225-4 (Paperback)

ISBN-13: 978-94-6475-225-0 (Paperback)

ISBN-10: 94-6475-223-8 (eBook)

ISBN-13: 978-94-6475-223-6 (eBook)

Printed by The International Committee in Search of Justice (ISJ)

https://www.isjcommittee.com/

"You see these dictators on their pedestals, surrounded by the bayonets of their soldiers and the truncheons of their police ... yet in their hearts there is unspoken fear. They are afraid of words and thoughts: words spoken abroad, thoughts stirring at home -- all the more powerful because forbidden -- terrify them. A little mouse of thought appears in the room, and even the mightiest potentates are thrown into panic."

- Winston S. Churchill

'Blood, Sweat and Tears'

This book is dedicated to all those who have strived for freedom and democracy in Iran for the past 120 years. We hope that they achieve their dream very soon.

ACKNOWLEDGEMENTS

My great thanks to Ambassador Lincoln Bloomfield Jr. and to Senator Giulio Terzi, for their friendship, wisdom, and support during the preparation of this book. Also, to my great friend of many decades Alejo Vidal Quadras, President of the ISJ. My gratitude, in addition, to the NCRI and PMOI/MEK, who fulfilled all my requests for documents, information and research materials, without any political consideration, in furtherance of my goal in writing this book.

Struan Stevenson

Chair In Search of Justice (ISJ) Committee on the Protection of Political Freedoms in Iran

Coordinator of the Campaign for Iran Change (CIC)

Glasgow, Scotland, January 2023

CONTENTS

LIST OF ILLUSTRATIONS

FOREWORD

As the world receives disturbing glimpses of the popular uprising gripping Iran, which has only intensified since the brutal September 2022 detention and killing of a 22-year-old woman by morality police over the positioning of her headscarf, many in the West seem at a loss to grasp the import of this momentous episode. Should not governments be focused on seeking agreement with the Tehran regime to curb its nuclear program in return for lifting economic sanctions? Should not diplomats be urging Iran and its neighbours to build on channels of dialogue and reconcile their differences? Are not the protestors' calls for an end to clerical rule a recipe for chaos, as other countries in the Middle East have experienced after their regimes have fallen? Is it not the case that there is no viable alternative to the fundamentalist Islamic dictatorship in Iran?

In this richly insightful and informative review of Iran's political history since the start of the 20th century, Struan Stevenson brings into painfully sharp focus the moral and geopolitical perils resulting from "Western political circles detached from the reality of Iran." While it should not require intellectual gymnastics to see that Iran's leaders have forfeited any pretence of a mandate to govern when security forces are beating and firing upon young women and even schoolgirls demanding relief from tyranny in over 300 cities, confusion endures. Hasn't Iran always had internal turmoil, from the 1953 coup against Mosaddegh to the 1979 revolution and the 2009 Green Movement protests? Hasn't the clerical regime always restored order when faced with protests over the past 44 years? As for who might try to restore calm and chart a future political course if the regime ever did fall from power, would not the late Shah's son Reza Pahlavi provide a more palatable option than, for example, the Mujahedin-e Khalq (MEK) and its umbrella organization, the National Council of Resistance of Iran (NCRI), which for decades has been labelled a Marxist, terrorist, cult-like organization?

For anyone who does not instantly recognize the righteous sarcasm in these questions, this book is a much-needed antidote, and a superb primer on Iran's turbulent contemporary political history.

For not only does Stevenson distil the relevant facts surrounding the country's most consequential political figures and civic challenges, but he illuminates the defining curse that for generations has thwarted the Iranian people's democratic aspirations, namely the corrupt and brutal alliance, tacit or explicit, of Iran's monarchists and clerics. It clearly needed illuminating, given the mulish reluctance of Western politicians and reporters to shoulder the duties imposed on them by an irredeemably malign global actor.

A member of the Scottish Conservative Party who for 15 years represented Scotland in the European Parliament, Struan Stevenson is the embodiment of democratic principles. His focus for many years on human rights abuses in the Middle East, principally Iraq and Iran, and his first-hand familiarity with the true nature and history of the MEK and NCRI, lend a depth of expertise on the subject matter and a moral gravitas that has made Stevenson a leading international critic of Iran's religious fascism, and an unimpeachable witness to the true nature and goals of Iran's organized resistance, the NCRI, led by Maryam Rajavi. The NCRI is, notwithstanding decades of regime-promoted propaganda to the contrary, a women-led, non-violent resistance movement dedicated to popular sovereignty, separation of religion and state, equal gender rights, an end to the death penalty, political legitimacy through the ballot box, commitment to international norms, and a non-nuclear Iran. No member has ever engaged in terrorism.

No longer can Western politicians – or correspondents, academics, and think-tank 'experts 'for that matter – afford to remain "detached from the reality of Iran." Given a quiz to test their knowledge of the 100 most salient facts in these pages on Iran's political evolution, most would fail miserably. In producing this stellar volume, Struan Stevenson has left them with no excuse.

Ambassador Lincoln Bloomfield Jr

Assistant Secretary of State-Political-Military Affairs (2001-2005)

Alexandria, VA, January 2023

PREFACE

"When dictatorship is a fact, revolution is a duty!" *Pascal Mercier*

This book is not a comprehensive history of Iran nor of its modern era. Rather the focus is on how two anachronistic institutions of Iranian society, namely the monarchy and the clergy, sometimes in collusion, sometimes in rivalry, have held Iranian society back from its full development and progress in the modern age and have led to dictatorship of one kind or the other. Their shared quality and ideology always stem from authoritarianism, either claiming to be the "Shadow of God" or the "Viceregent of God" on earth, and the denial of political, economic, and civil liberties to citizens that form the bedrock of a free and democratic society based on rule of law.

Since the mid-1800s, the awakening of Iranians and their determined drive to join the modern era began with attempted reforms to industrialize and modernize the country by Amir Kabir (Mirza Taghi Khan-e Farahani) which was thwarted by the Qajar absolute monarch and his corrupt court at the behest of the British empire.

Iranians decried the monarchy's vast and enslaving concessions to foreign interests and engaged in a rule of law revolution (Constitutional Revolution of 1906) to limit the absolute power of the monarchy and establish oversight of a legislative branch (Majlis). The revolution was thwarted by Tsarist Russian intervention, the onset of the Great War, and subsequent British interference to restore absolute monarchy.

The oil nationalization project of the democratic government of Mohammad Mosaddegh in the 1950s pushed back the monarchy to make Iranians masters of their own country but was illegally overthrown by a foreign instigated coup d'état supported by the reactionary clerics and their mobs to again restore absolute monarchy.

When the Shah engaged in reforms from the top to push Iran to industrialize and expand oil production, all the while denying awakened Iranians their inalienable right to political, economic, and civil liberties, Iranians sought to reclaim their rights, but were faced with a brutal police-military crackdown led by the Shah's secret police (SAVAK). The Shah went so far as to establish one-party rule and called on all Iranians opposed to his authoritarianism to either leave Iran or endure prison.[1] And so it was that the 1979 revolution took shape. With democratically inclined leaders and intellectuals all imprisoned or executed by the monarchy, the clergy rode the anti-monarchy wave in society to victory and usurped the leadership of that momentous revolution.

Now, after 44 years, the absolute religious rule of the clergy with theoretical claims to Islam, albeit opposed by intellectuals and laymen of faith, has revealed itself as another incarnation of that same impediment to democratic development of Iranian society: ruthless dictatorship, and disregard of the rule of law based on universal human rights.

As this book was being written in the summer of 2022, Iran was rapidly gripped with another cataclysmic uprising in September. The refrain "this time it is different" could be heard from every corner of Iranian society and intelligentsia and even from foreign observers and students of Iranian affairs. The regime lacks any legitimacy, has lost cohesion at the top and among its security establishment and forces, and is engaged in criminal negligence and corruption in the management of Iran's economy. The mullahs' regime is facing widespread and unprecedented dissent among the populace and is confronted by unwavering and uncompromising calls for its overthrow. Abroad too, the policy of appeasing this regime is rapidly losing traction as the European Parliament called overwhelmingly for Iran's Revolutionary Guards (IRGC) to be

---

[1]. "If there is anyone who refuses to join this political party ... he belongs in a prison in Iran ... or if he wants, he can, with pleasure, leave to wherever he wants." (Mohammad Reza Pahlavi's speech as published in Ettelaat newspaper, March 3, 1975).

blacklisted as a terrorist organisation in Europe as the book was going to press in late January.

Iran is once again in a revolutionary situation. In times past, Iranians have been robbed of experiencing democracy and becoming a true republic of the people, for the people, and by the people, by various foreign interventions, coups, and monarchist and clerical machinations. This time around, a viable democratic alternative with no vestiges of the monarchy or the clergy, has grown in opposition to both. A vision presented by Maryam Rajavi and her Ten Point Plan for the future of Iran, together with the international and domestic solidarity assembled by the National Council of Resistance of Iran (NCRI), heralds new hope that authoritarian outcomes can be averted, and a truly democratic republic can be realized.

INTRODUCTION

As the Iranian people strive to defeat the medieval religious dictatorship of the mullahs in Iran, it is evermore imperative that we do not lose sight of the larger historical perspective in which this struggle has been shaped. The Iranian political landscape and society are imbued with memories of a 120-year struggle to achieve some form of democratic governance and open society that is so often taken for granted in countries with established democratic rule. This century-long effort has at times been waged against despotic Shahs (monarchs) and now against clerics claiming absolute theocratic rule.

Both the monarchy and the theocratic dictatorship deny universal human rights, claim authority as "Shadow of God" (the Shahs) or "Vicegerent of God" (clerical despots) on earth, consider the people to be immature and in need of guardians, and derive their legitimacy from sources other than the ballot box and democratic rule of law. Both have committed gross violations of human rights such as arbitrary detentions, summary trials, cruel and inhuman punishment, torture, and political executions. Both have effectively instituted one-party rule, denied pluralism, suppressed many segments of society, denied freedom of speech or association, prohibited a free press, and disenfranchised citizens. One has come to hold foreign interests above that of the nation in the case of the monarchy, and the other has abused the faith and religiosity of the people to plunder their wealth, to instigate hatred, sectarian violence, and foreign adventurism, under the rubric of religious war and expansion, to the detriment of the nation.

This book, comprised of 23 chapters, attempts to chronicle a concise history of the Pahlavi monarchs who were ousted by popular revolution in 1979, and the religious dictatorship that took its place after Ruhollah Khomeini usurped the leadership of the anti-monarchic revolution. The first three chapters delve into the illegitimate rise of the Pahlavi monarchs through brutal repression and foreign intervention and the years preceding the 1979 revolution. The next couple of chapters deal with how the clergy, with Khomeini at the forefront, tolerated and left intact by the Shah, contrary to the decimation of democratic forces, hijacked the revolution and thwarted its deals of freedom.

The monarchic remnants of the previous regime are unmasked in the next chapter and the resistance movement to the theocratic regime is described in the following chapter. The regime's destructive domestic and international policies are covered in chapters 9 to 17. The consequences of the regime's crimes and its appeasement by Western governments is discussed in chapters 18 and 19. The regime's concerted and vicious disinformation campaign against its opposition and its use of cyberwar are examined in chapters 20 and 21.

The last two chapters deal with the current national uprising in Iran and prospects for a democratic outcome. The 1979 revolution against the Pahlavi Shah started in January 1978 with the first bloody crackdown of demonstrations, and lasted for 13 months, culminating in the flight of the Shah and the overthrow of his regime. This revolution, after over four decades of organized resistance, is now in its fifth month at the time of writing with protesters calling for "Death to Khamenei", the supreme leader of the regime, and wholesale regime change, undaunted by the level of repression. This time around, the regime, having failed to decimate or eliminate the Iranian Resistance movement physically or politically, is facing its inevitable downfall at the hands of a popular uprising inspired by this decades-long resistance and the vision it presents for a free, democratic, pluralistic, nuclear-free Iran, with separation of religion and state.

Chapter One

HOW A COSSACK COLONEL ROSE TO BE A PERSIAN KING

Reza Khan, who was born in the village of Alasht in Mazandaran province in 1878, was taken to Tehran and later joined the Cossack Brigade as a young soldier. Reza Khan was illiterate and has often been described as a local bully[2] who served as a leader of religious bands in public ceremonies led by local clergy and served as their community enforcer (referred to as *luti* [3] in Persian).

In 1903, Reza served as a guard and servant to the Dutch consul general in Tehran. With an ambitious and ruthless demeanour, he rose to the rank of sergeant, first lieutenant, colonel, and then brigadier general in the Persian Cossack Brigade.

The creation of a small Cossack cavalry regiment, based on the Russian Imperial model by Naser al-Din Shah (a Qajar shah), in 1879 began as a token of friendship to the Russian tsar to counterbalance the tilt toward the British in the Shah's court at the time. The regiment later expanded to become the Cossack Brigade and its commander and officers were Russians who were entirely loyal to Imperial Russia and did the tsar's bidding in Iran by protecting the Qajar throne while exposing Iranians to the overbearing conduct of the Cossack commanders and their troops who were from the Caucasus and Iranian.

---

[2] Milani, Abbas. 2011. *The Shah*, London: Macmillan, p. 14. In his book Mission for My Country, Reza Shah's son, Mohammad Reza Pahlavi, describes his father as "one of the most frightening men" he had ever known.

[3] "Luti people - Wikipedia." En. https://en.wikipedia.org/wiki/Luti_people#:~:text=Luti%20people%20(Persian%3A%20%D9%84%D9%88%D8%B7%DB%8C),numbers%20exist%20on%20their%20population.

The Brigade violently intervened in the burgeoning Iranian democratic process and constitutional revolution of 1906 by forcefully dissolving the first Majlis[4] (parliament) and plunged Iran into a political crisis that lasted until 1921 when Reza Khan, now the commander of the Cossack force, led a coup with British backing, against a weak Qajar shah who had lost his Russian imperial patron after the rise of the Bolsheviks in newly constituted Soviet Russia.

Under the rule of the Qajar dynasty, foreign interference by Russia and Britain had ravaged Iran, and drove the nation into financial and economic ruin, political crisis, and internal confrontations. The Qajars, weak in the face of foreign influence, while aggressively repressive towards Iranian citizens, colluded with Russia and the reactionary Iranian clergy against a nascent democratic movement in Iran that had succeeded in imposing constitutional limits on the monarchy, to claw back it's absolute power after 1906.

As a testament to the times in Iran, William Morgan Shuster, an American civil servant and banker with integrity, who was hired by the Iranian Majlis in 1911 to set the country's finances in order as treasurer-general, denounced the imperial powers interference in Iran in his book "The Strangling of Persia"[5] in 1912. Shuster's sincere efforts to aid Iranians was short-lived and he was quickly forced out by Russian threats. He dedicated his book to the Persian people and wrote in the foreword on 30 April 1912, "The Constitutionalists of Modern Persia will not have lived, struggled, and in many instances died, entirely in vain, if the destruction of the Persian sovereignty shall have sharpened somewhat the civilized world's realization of the spirit of international brigandage which marked the *welt-politik* of the year 1911."

Shuster wrote, "Despite the brilliant success of the Persian Nationalists in forcing the deposition and exile from the country of the late Shah [the Qajar Shah Mohammad Ali] after his repeated

---

[4] Cronin, Stephanie. 1997. *The Army and Creation of the Pahlavi State in Iran, 1921-1926*. I.B.Tauris. p. 61.
[5] Shuster, William Morgan. 1912. *The Strangling of Persia*.

violations of his promises and oaths to faithfully observe the Constitution and the rights of his people, the prospects of Persia being able to evolve from the complicated situation confronting her, a reasonable stable and orderly government, were far from encouraging."[6]

By 1921, Iran ravaged by wars waged by foreign belligerents on its soil, interference by Russia and Britain, a plunder of its resources and revenues under highly exploitative concessions by weak Qajar kings to seemingly private European firms, was steaming toward social and political upheaval that instigated a resurgence of enlightenment called the "awakening of Iranians".

Popular movements in the north and east,[7] a vibrant press, a bourgeoning merchant class, proliferation of modern schools and education, and a growing awareness that Iran must move into modernity and remove the shackles of ignorance and superstition imposed on it by the clergy and impediments and undue taxation and plunder of the monarchy, as well as the "brigandage" of imperial powers, all of whom aligned against change to prolong the status quo, were fermenting in Iranian society.

Having supported Iranian constitutionalists in the months leading up to the 1906 Constitutional Revolution, the British imperial order found the "Iranian awakening" in 1921 unsavoury, and after many years of competition with Russia saw an opportunity to advance its commercial, political, and grand strategy in Iran, to the detriment of Iranian democrats. Hoping to exploit the William Knox D'Arcy oil concession, enhance the security of British India, further its Great War defeat of Germany, and supplant waning Russian influence after the Bolshevik revolution, Britain took a wrong turn in Iran.

Reza Khan was promoted to commander of the Cossack Brigade by British General Edmund Ironside in January of 1921, and under

---

[6] Ibid, p li

[7] Among notable democratic examples were the "Jungle Movement" led by Mirza Kuchak Khan in the north, and the Khorasan movement led by Mohammad-Taqi Pessian in Khorosan province in northeastern Iran.

British direction, he marched and occupied Tehran on 21 February in a coup that effectively nipped the Iranian democratic movement in the bud.

On the morning of 21 February, ordinary Iranians saw a nine-article communique signed by "Reza, Chief of His Majesty's Cossack Division and Military Commander of Tehran", posted on public thoroughfares proclaiming in ominous terms "I command" and ordering the people of Tehran to be "quiet and obedient to military commands". Reza Khan instituted martial law and fashioned himself a "strongman", promising to save Iran from crisis.

Reza Khan, initially appointed Minister of War, quickly took control, becoming prime minister in 1923. He forced a now subservient Iranian Majlis (parliament) to depose the absent monarch, Ahmad Shah, in 1925 and to elect himself as Shah, effectively vesting sovereignty in the newly named Pahlavi dynasty.

Figure 1 - Reza Khan

After his coronation as the Shah of Iran in 1926, he set about consolidating his hold in Iran and putting his imprint on the country. He forcefully confiscated large estates estimated to be over 3 million acres throughout Iran, making his household the richest in the country.[8] He confiscated the Iranian monarchy's riches in emeralds, rubies, diamonds, gold, silver, and art. He suppressed national and ethnic minorities and movements, bullied the nascent Iranian press and intelligentsia, violated the Iranian constitution of 1906 and parliament's will with impunity, engaged in compulsory unveiling of women in traditional Iranian communities, and so many other authoritarian injustices that made him infamous as "Reza the Bully". [9]

This personal trait came to be Reza Khan's undoing. While he came to power in a very British coup,[10] his tendencies led him to align with Hitler's Nazi Germany during the Second World War. His strategy of playing off one side against the other fell apart when Britain and the Soviets joined forces against the Germans. Fearing that the Shah would cooperate with Hitler, the two allies jointly occupied Iran in 1941, also inviting 30,000 American personnel after the US joined the war, forcing Reza Shah to abdicate and hand over the throne to his son, Mohammad Reza Pahlavi.

---

[8] According to author Hossein Makki in his book "A 20-year History," these predominantly highly sought-after real estate properties were confiscated in Gilan, Mazandaran, Tonekabon, Nour, and numerous other locations. By the time he was deposed, he is believed to have forcibly seized 44,000 land titles from their owners. Writing in the Washington Post on October 1, 1941, American journalist for the Associated Press and Pulitzer Prize winner Daniel De Luce reported that Reza Shah had the equivalent of anywhere between $20 million to $300 million dollars in his bank accounts.

[9] According to the book "The Past Informs the Future," it is estimated that in the course of Reza Shah's reign, 24,000 people were killed at Qasr Prison alone, most of whom were political activists, intellectuals, and ethnic minorities. (Gozashte Cheraghe Rahe Ayandeh Ast, Tehran: Niloufar,2001, p. 158).

[10] Brysac, Shareen Blair. "A Very British Coup – How Reza Shah Won and Lost His Throne| World Policy Journal | Duke University Press.".

Chapter Two

MOHAMMAD REZA SHAH PAHLAVI

THE MAKING OF AN AUTOCRAT

So began a turbulent period in Iran's long history. Reza Khan handed over his ill begotten wealth and crown to his eldest son on his way out of the Imperial palace. Born in 1919 in Tehran, his son Mohammad Reza was the third of eleven children. As much as Reza Khan was a bully, the new Shah was a vacillating and timid soul before he could gain his footing at exercising his newfound power.

In his memoirs, Mohammad Reza referred to his father's violent temperament, adding that he was "one of the most frightening men I've ever known". Growing up under Reza Khan's dominant and scary shadow, Mohammad Reza was a deeply insecure boy. According to the seminal book "The Shah," Mohammad Reza described his father in private conversations as "a thuggish Cossack" who did little as king. [11] The younger Pahlavi ascended to the throne on September 16, 1941. The turning point in the Shah's reign seemed in many ways like his father's: another foreign-sponsored coup (in 1953) that brought him back to power after he was run out of the country by a popular uprising.

As Shah, Mohammad Reza was determined to pursue a pro-Western foreign policy, encouraging inward investment and economic development in Iran. He encouraged the Americans in particular, who tended to regard Iran as a laboratory for experiments in social science and their brand of democracy. During the war years, Iran was in the extraordinary position of having been occupied by all three of the great allied powers, who were keen to preserve a supply route to Russia. However, Stalin, seizing the

---

[11] Milani, Abbas. 2011. *The Shah*, London: Macmillan, p. 15.

opportunity to extend Soviet authority and territory, occupied what he called a 'zone of influence' in the five provinces adjacent to Russia in northern Iran. In this he found support from the leftist Tudeh Party in the Iranian Majlis, who argued for extensive oil concessions to be granted to the Soviets. In doing so, they alienated liberals and nationalists alike, who feared Russian encroachment on Iranian sovereignty. It was during this hotbed of democratic politics in the early years of the Shah's reign, that his taste for autocracy and authoritarian rule began to develop. Lavishing his attention on the army, which he saw as his personal fiefdom, he gradually began to curtail the powers of parliament and to curb the influence of the burgeoning press. There were dozens of newspapers in Tehran at that time, though most of the citizens were illiterate. Many of them were simply the mouthpiece of factional political movements.

Figure 2 - The autocratic Mohammad Reza Shah Pahlavi

The Shah increasingly came to exploit crises as an excuse and opportunity to curtail Iran's political parties and press freedom. In this he found ready support from the mullahs, who were keen to back the monarchy. Since the 1979 revolution, the mullahs have gone to great lengths to portray themselves as outright opponents of the Pahlavi dynasty, but this was not the case. The clergy and the Shah were close allies. The young Shah endeared himself to the mullahs by reversing his father's ban on women wearing the veil in public and he made several trips to the holy city of Qom to consult the Ayatollahs.

But by the 1950s he had clashed with Mohammad Mossadegh, an ardent Iranian nationalist and member of the Majlis who spearheaded legislation in the Majlis calling for the nationalization of the Iranian oil industry, ending almost 50 years of British monopoly over Iran's petroleum excavation, extraction, research, marketing, and sales.

In March 1951, Mosaddegh succeeded in passing his bill in parliament to nationalize the assets of the Anglo-Iranian Oil Company (AIOC), later known as British Petroleum (BP). William D'Arcy, a British businessman, had purchased the right to exploit Iran's oilfields in 1901, paying the country's ruling family £20,000 together with a promise of a 16% share of annual profits. Following the First World War, the British government bought 52.5% of the company's shares, and set about converting its naval fleet from coal to oil. By the 1940s, AIOC was paying more in tax annually to the British government than in royalties to Iran, infuriating nationalists like Mosaddegh. For millions of Iranians, he symbolized Iranian sovereignty and patriotism.

Seeing Mosaddegh's influence and popularity grow, the Shah had no option but to appoint him as premier in April 1951. During his short tenure in office (April 1951-August 1953) he stood up to the Shah's illegitimate interference in the government's affairs and earned the enmity of the Shah and his court. Two years of conflict and tension commenced, coming to a head in 1953, when the Shah attempted to dismiss Mosaddegh, but the ensuing mass protests by his supporters forced the Shah to flee the country.

With the covert assistance of the Americans and the British in what was dubbed as "Operation Ajax", Mohammad Reza was restored to power in a coup a few days later and Mosaddegh was arrested by coup leaders, charged with treason, and sentenced to three years imprisonment. After his release he was kept under house arrest for the rest of his life. It was an ominous sign of the growing autocracy of the Shah.

Figure 3 - Mohammad Mosaddegh

It could be argued that Mohammad Mosaddegh's illegal ouster from the premiership by a foreign coup in support of the Shah as dictator of Iran, snuffed out the last vestiges of Iran's democratic process and ended any hopes of parliamentary reforms in Iran. The Shah and his court were now seen by Iran's young intelligentsia as serving foreign interests and powers engaged in economic and political exploitation of the country. [12]

Once more in charge, Mohammad Reza Shah replaced the nationalized oil company with an international oil consortium that now shared Iran's oil riches with American companies. With US support he launched two major initiatives to prepare Iran for integration into the global market and entry of primarily US conglomerates. The first, 'The White Revolution', involved token reforms such as giving women the right to vote, improving compensation for industrial workers, and distributing land confiscated from the old aristocracy to peasant farmers. The reform from above was meant to preserve traditional power patterns and safeguard the Shah's rule from a young generation that increasingly sought political freedoms and social justice.

The land reforms in practise supplanted nobles and landlords into a new more powerful group of commercial farmers. The Pahlavi family itself became the most prominent of the new commercial farmers. The peasantry as a whole did not acquire land. Only roughly half of the rural population received any land, and many of the people who did receive land did not receive enough to sustain themselves.[13] Not able to survive economically, the peasantry was driven into destitution. This in turn caused a huge migration to urban centres, creating Iran's new urban poor who would serve as cheap labour for the Shah's industrialization plans.

His second initiative, in response to American demands for more political openness in Iran, involved the creation of his Rastakhiz (Resurgence) Party, which was entirely controlled by the Shah's regime and became Iran's only legal political party, effectively turning the country into a one-party state. The youth wing of the

---

[12] In December 1953, in protest to the Shah as a puppet of foreign powers, students in Tehran went on strike. The Shah's police opened fire on students at the University of Tehran, killing three of them. To this day, December 7 (16 Azar in Iranian calendar) is marked as "Student Day" in universities across Iran.

[13] Siavoshi, Sussan. 1990. *Liberal Nationalism in Iran: The failure of a movement*. Boulder, Colorado: Westview Press, p. 28.

Rastakhiz Party launched a massive anti-profiteering campaign against the bazaari merchants, identifying them as "enemies of the state." This immediately served to alienate a large proportion of the population.

In 1958, the Americans had helped to form the dreaded SAVAK secret police with the help of the CIA, and the Shah began a ruthless crackdown on opposition movements, all the while raising the spectre of Communists and radical Islamists.

Figure 4 - SAVAK SECRET POLICE emblem

To this day, one of the Shah's notorious prisons where detainees were routinely tortured, has been retained as a museum in Tehran. Ebrat prison (Komiteh Moshtarak) was reserved for political prisoners who opposed the Shah and his American backed monarchy. It was here prisoners were stripped naked, tied to beds, and whipped with cables.[14] Electric shocks were administered to sensitive parts of the body. Prisoners could also be locked in a metal cage with a gas burner underneath, known as 'the hot box'. This prison remained in use after the 1979 revolution, serving as a torture chamber for opponents of Ayatollah Khomeini until 2000.

---

[14] "The shah of Iran retains his benevolent image despite the highest rate of death penalties in the world, no valid system of civilian courts and a history of torture which is beyond belief," Amnesty International said in a 1974-75 report.

Figure 5 - Ebrat Prison is today a museum.

Chapter Three

THE ADVENT OF A DICTATORSHIP

By the early 1970s, there were growing signs that the Shah's twin passions of modernization and political oppression were beginning to backfire. The Shah's ban on all political groups apart from the Rastakhiz Party, created disillusionment and disenchantment amongst Iran's then 25 million population. His attempts to westernize Iran without consulting the people led to discontent. Although by his efforts he had helped to build Iran's middle class, his refusal to allow them a say in national affairs caused deep resentment and created huge disparity and more poverty. An enriched segment of society invested in the Shah's rule, and then a middle and majority lower class were denied freedom.

The Shah's obsession with Western values was slowly driving his people back to reclaiming their religion and his brutal crackdown on dissenting voices fuelled demands for his overthrow. Ayatollah Ruhollah Khomeini, exiled to Najaf, Iraq, in 1964 and publicly silent until one year before the Shah's overthrow, used his time in Iraq and then France to rally support for his Islamic fundamentalist principles from mullahs and students, while inside Iran resistance to the dictatorship steadily grew.

Against this backdrop, in the autumn of 1965, three young university graduates, Mohammad Hanifnejad, Saied Mohsen and Ali-Asghar Badizadegan, set up the People's Mojahedin Organisation of Iran/Mojahedin-e Khalq (PMOI/MEK), a political movement formed to oppose the corrupt and oppressive dictatorship of Reza Shah Pahlavi and the absolute rule of the monarch. The PMOI would grow to become by far the largest and most active political movement in Iranian history.[15]

Figure 6 - Mohammad Hanifnejad, Ali-Asghar Badizadegan, Saied Mohsen.

In the 1970s, however, a brutal crackdown on the organisation and its members by the SAVAK secret police resulted in the execution of the PMOI/MEK's original founders, almost the entirety of its leadership and the imprisonment of most of its members and

[15] When Massoud Rajavi, the organisation's then Secretary General, ran for president in 1980, his candidacy was endorsed by "an impressive array of independent organizations ... The Mojahedin had become the vanguards of the secular opposition to the Islamic Republic." (See Abrahamian, Ervand. 1989. *The Iranian Mojahedin*, Yale University Press, p. 198). After Khomeini vetoed Rajavi's candidacy, the French daily Le Monde wrote, "According to diverse estimates, had Imam Khomeini not vetoed his candidacy in the presidential election last January, Mr. Rajavi, would have gotten several million votes." (See Eric Roleau, a report from Tehran, Le Monde, March 29, 1980).

supporters, including Massoud Rajavi, then a member of the PMOI/MEK leadership. Massoud Rajavi was a graduate of political law from Tehran University and had joined the PMOI/MEK when he was 18. He was only spared execution because of the efforts of his elder brother Professor Kazem Rajavi, a renowned human rights advocate who spearheaded an international campaign in the West, which included securing the support of Francois Mitterrand and several other international leaders and human rights organisations, including Amnesty International.[16]

While Massoud Rajavi and the rest of the PMOI/MEK's leading cadres were in prison, the organisation suffered an internal setback. In the years 1972-1975, several individuals, including a member who had escaped prison and gained some notoriety among the opposition, took advantage of the organisation's leadership vacuum and criticized the original leadership's decidedly progressive interpretation of Islam. He undemocratically announced a change to the organisation's ideology and direction along Marxist lines. The remaining members outside prison, who strongly rejected the betrayal of the PMOI/MEK's founders and their vision for a future Iran, vigorously opposed this Marxist coup within the organisation.[17] But the Marxist faction engaged in several armed attacks against American personnel stationed in Iran as a way to shore up its power over the organisation.[18] The faction even murdered several high-ranking members of the organisation who were attempting to prevent the coup.

---

[16] Bloomfield, Lincoln Jr. 2013. *The Mujahedin-e Khalq (MEK)*, University of Baltimore, p. 14.

[17] Ibid., p. 18.

[18] This splinter group "denounced the Islamic orientation of the organization in favor of a Marxist-Leninist line and expelled those members who did not adhere to it. The Marxist Leninist faction went so far as to use terrorist methods such as setting fire to Shareef Vaqefi, a leader of the Islamic faction, in order to gain control of the organization... Advocating armed urban guerrilla operations, in 1975, the Marxist-Leninist Mujahedin carried out several terrorist actions, among them the assassination of Col. Turner, Col. Schaefer, and later Gen. Price." (The Middle East Journal, Vol. 41, No. 2, Spring 1987).

According to international experts who have closely examined the events of the 1970s, these armed activities were aimed at gaining the upper hand and silencing any opposition to the change in ideology and strategy of the organisation. Massoud Rajavi, although in prison, wrote a book criticizing these deviationists, strongly condemning these individuals and their actions. He went on to play a vital role in returning the organization to its true and original founding principles and ideology.[19] The PMOI/MEK can therefore in no way be held responsible for actions by the Marxist faction in which it played no part.

Once released from prison in 1979, Massoud Rajavi and other senior PMOI/MEK members set about restructuring the organization. Because of the group's nationalist outlook, democratic values and modern, progressive view of Islam, they were the natural front-runners in the 1979 revolution. It was because of their tolerant and progressive interpretation of Islam that the PMOI/MEK provided ideological inspiration to the millions of Iranians whose nationwide protests ultimately brought down the Shah of Iran in 1979.

The PMOI/MEK wanted a secular government, democratic elections and universal suffrage to be the basis of political legitimacy.[20] Their interpretation of Islam and what they aspired to for a future Iran was, however, in stark contrast to the intentions of Ayatollah Khomeini, a fanatical Shi'a cleric who had recently returned to Iran from exile.[21] The Shah had exiled Khomeini in 1964, due to his

---

[19] People's Mojahedin Organization of Iran, "Educational Analyses of the Statement of the pseudo-Leftist Opportunists," spring 1979.

[20] Abrahamian writes, "In criticizing the regime's political record, the Mojahedin moved the issue of democracy to center stage. They argued that the regime had broken all the democratic promises made during the revolution; that an attack on any group was an attack on all groups; that the issue of democracy was of 'fundamental importance'". See Abrahamian, op. cit. 209.

[21] In his first public speech after the revolution, published in Kayhan, January 25, 1979, p. 4, Massoud Rajavi said, "Our Islam is not the type that restricts struggle to a special force or group. Did not our leader [Imam Hussein] say, if you do not believe in any religion, at least be free minded?" The French daily Le Monde wrote at the time, Rajavi's ideological and political message was that "freedom is the essence of

increasing prominence as a religious leader, and his opposition to the Shah's pro-Western program that Khomeini had spearheaded from an antimodern and traditionalist perspective.

Figure 7 - Massoud Rajavi

---

evolution and the principal message of Islam and revolution" (Le Monde, Paris, March 29, 1980).

Chapter Four

HIJACKING THE REVOLUTION

The overthrow of the Shah in the 1979 revolution was hailed by the Iranian people as a deliverance from cruel oppression, although it took the West by surprise. At the time, the Shah had the largest, most powerful, and best-equipped army in the region. The rise in the price of oil had improved the quality of life for some Iranians. However, the West, including the US, failed to grasp two major issues, despite their extensive presence in Iran at the time. First, there was a lack of freedom in a country whose people were dying for it; and second, a large proportion of the Iranian population was still suffering from poverty. The gulf between rich and poor had widened.

The monarchy's relationship with the clergy was a complex one that played an important role in the events of the 1979 revolution. Historically, the clergy, independent from the monarchy, had shared a symbiotic relationship with the latter. The monarchy derived its "divine" claim to legitimacy from the clergy, and the clergy derived its social power and wealth from the monarchy's acquiescence. The two institutions were a major impediment to the formation of a developed civic society based on democratic values and human rights. Their role in blocking genuine reform in Iran during the Constitutional Revolution in 1906 and afterwards, [22] and in plotting to oust the democratic nationalist government of

---

[22] Sheikh Fazlullah Nouri, a traditionalist Shia Muslim cleric who turned against the Constitutionalists in 1906. Nouri was honored by Khomeini and his followers who considered him a martyr in the fight of Islamist conservatives against democracy.

Mohammad Mosaddegh in 1953,[23] defined the circumstances that led up to the 1979 revolution.

The Shah had initially shown fidelity to religious customs and leaned on the clergy during the first two decades of his rule. He sought to keep the support of the Grand Ayatollah Hossein Borujerdi who died in 1961. After the Shah's "White Revolution" he displayed anti-religious attitudes that angered traditional Iranian society but tried to keep the clergy under his tutelage at the same time. The clergy, with some exceptions, tried to stay in the Shah's favour and maintained widespread relations with SAVAK. While most political dissidents were imprisoned or executed in the 1970s, the clerical establishment was mostly left untouched as the anti-Shah demonstrations of 1978 started.

After widespread demonstrations against his rule, the Shah fled on 16 January 1979, never to return. Massoud Rajavi, the leader of the PMOI/MEK was freed from political prison only 4 days later. By that time, Khomeini and his clerical network had taken advantage of the vacuum created by the Shah's lengthy dictatorship and the elimination of all democratic opposition groups. The Shah's last prime minister was emasculated and Khomeini hijacked control of the revolution and took power in Tehran. The lack of democratic institutions and public knowledge about the true nature of Khomeini contributed to his position going unchallenged at the time. He was seen as a spiritual leader who had no interest in material life or in engaging in the day-to-day affairs of the country. Indeed, he promised that this would be the case.

When Khomeini returned to Iran in triumph on 1st February 1979, after the Shah had fled, he was welcomed by an estimated crowd of up to five-million people. Like most observers in the West, the Iranian people believed that this elderly, bearded, holy man, would

---

[23] Ayatollah Abol-Ghasem Kashani, a Shia Marja (leader) initially joined the nationalist prime minister Mohammad Mosaddegh in opposing British domination of Iran's oil industry but later turned against him and supported the 1953 coup d'état that brought down Mosaddegh's government by commanding his luti supporters to provide the muscle for "Operation Ajax".

restore peace, stability, and prosperity to their nation. How wrong they were. Little did they realise that Khomeini was a psychopathic murderer intent on plunging their country into a fundamentalist cauldron, exterminating anyone who stood in his way. However, having secured the support of the people by taking advantage of their religious feelings, he reneged on his promises, and instead of setting up a constituent assembly representing the people, and instructing it to write the new constitution, he set up an Assembly of Experts, which was essentially made up of clerics. This assembly introduced a constitution based on the principle of 'Velayat-e-faqih' - the absolute rule of the clergy, a theory about which Khomeini had written before. He gave himself the title of Supreme Leader and established the Guardians' Council, which holds absolute power and controls everything, including all legislative acts, to ensure they are in accordance with strict interpretation of Sharia and the Quran.

Khomeini appointed himself God's representative on earth, changing Iranian society overnight and giving birth to what is now known as Islamic fundamentalism. His medieval belief that his authority came directly from God enabled him to rule over a fascist theocracy that could imprison, torture, maim and execute at will, ruling by fear and violence and defending these excesses by stating they were the will of God. Similar to the 'divine right of Kings' which bathed Europe in blood for centuries, this discredited anachronism plunged the population of forward-looking and highly civilized Iranians back to the Middle Ages, where women could be stoned to death and men hanged from cranes in town squares because they were guilty of 'waging war on God.'

The PMOI/MEK fiercely opposed this undemocratic seizure of power by the mullahs and refused to take part in the referendum on the 'Velayat-e-faqih' constitution. Massoud Rajavi was tipped to win election as the Islamic Republic's first president, but Khomeini banned him from standing on the grounds that he had refused to accept the Velayat-e-faqih constitution.[24] A report prepared by the British Foreign Office describes this period: "The MKO [PMOI/MEK] played a major part in the revolution and for two years thereafter was an important element in the internal power struggle. It boycotted the referendum on the Islamic Republic's constitution and Rajavi was forced to withdraw his candidacy for the post of President of the Republic when Khomeini said that only those who voted for the constitution could be candidates. Rajavi stood for election to the majlis [Iranian Parliament] in 1980 but was not elected – almost certainly because of ballot rigging.'

[24] Khomeini banned Rajavi and other MEK candidates for office on the basis of their refusal to support his new constitution. Le Monde's correspondent wrote on March 29, 1980, that Rajavi would have received "several million votes" including support from "religious and ethnic minorities ... a good part of the female vote ... and the young" had his candidacy not been disallowed because the PMOI did not vote for the regime's constitution that was based on velayat-e faqih and the mullahs' absolute rule.

Chapter Five

KHOMEINI'S REIGN OF TERROR

Infuriated by the PMOI/MEK's stance against him, Ayatollah Khomeini ordered a brutal and bloody crackdown on members, supporters and sympathisers of the PMOI/MEK in what has been described as the 'reign of terror'.[25] According to a decree by Khomeini, 'the Mojahedin of Iran are infidels and worse than blasphemers . . . They have no right to life.' Since then, the PMOI/MEK have been the principal victims of human rights violations in Iran. Over the past four decades, 120,000 of its members and supporters have been executed. Dozens more have been assassinated outside of Iran. The execution, imprisonment, and torture of PMOI/MEK members, supporters and their families continue unabated to this day.

In the summer of 1988 alone, some 30,000 PMOI/MEK political prisoners were executed in prisons throughout Iran. They were led to the gallows and buried in mass graves in secret locations.[26] In a final act of barbarity, the Iranian regime has for the past 4 decades deprived the families of the victims with the knowledge of the final resting place of their loved ones. To this day, families meet in secret throughout Iran, in search of the remains of their loved ones. The UN now has irrefutable evidence of the massacre of political prisoners in the summer of 1988. It was an atrocity that must rank as a crime against humanity and one of the most horrific mass

---

[25] Shortly after the revolution, on June 25, 1980, Khomeini pointed his finger at the PMOI/MEK and said they are "worse than infidels." Even the organisation's health clinics soon came under attack. There were more deaths and injuries, and thousands of arrests (Mojahed, No. 115, 9 April 1981).

[26] Amnesty International, "IRAN: BLOOD-SOAKED SECRETS: WHY IRAN'S 1988 PRISON MASSACRES ARE ONGOING CRIMES AGAINST HUMANITY", December 4, 2018, Index number: MDE 13/9421/2018.

murders of the late twentieth century.[27] The mass executions, in jails across Iran, were carried out based on a fatwa by Ayatollah Khomeini. A 'Death Committee' of four senior officials approved all the executions. Khomeini instructed that the executions should be carried out in haste and that even pregnant women should not be spared.

Figure 8 – Regime founder - Ayatollah Ruhollah Khomeini

Kangaroo courts were set up in Tehran and in 100 other cities across Iran and PMOI/MEK political prisoners were hauled in front of a Sharia judge who demanded to know if they supported the Mojahedin. Those who defiantly said yes were sentenced to immediate execution. These sham trials took on average 3 minutes. It was estimated that 30,000 political prisoners were hanged in batches of ten, every fifteen minutes from dawn to dusk, between August & December 1988.

[27] Robertson, Geoffrey QC. 2009. *The Massacre of Political Prisoners in Iran, 1988*, Washington, DC, Abdorraham Bouramand Foundation.

The truth about this horrific genocide was revealed when the son of Grand Ayatollah Hossein-Ali Montazeri, the former Deputy Supreme Leader of the Islamic Republic and the nominated successor to Ayatollah Khomeini, published a previously unknown audiotape in which Montazeri acknowledged that the massacre had taken place and had been ordered at the highest levels.[28] In the electrifying tape, Montazeri can be heard telling a meeting of the 'Death Committee' in 1988 that they were responsible for a crime against humanity. He says: "The greatest crime committed during the reign of the Islamic Republic, for which history will condemn us, has been committed by you. Your names will in the future be etched in the annals of history as criminals." Because he had dared to complain, Montazeri was removed as Khomeini's successor and detained under house arrest for the rest of his life.

Figure 9 - Grand Ayatollah Hossein Ali Montazeri

[28] "Audio file revives calls for inquiry into massacre of Iran political prisoners," The Guardian, August 11, 2016.

During the 1988 massacre, anyone who stood by his/her affiliation to the PMOI (MEK) was sent to the gallows. According to an Amnesty International report, some of the questions posed to the prisoners were as follows: [29]

- *Are you prepared to denounce the PMOI and its leadership?*
- *Are you willing to join the armed forces of the Islamic Republic and fight against the PMOI?*
- *Are you willing to hang a member of the PMOI?*
- *Will you spy on former comrades and "co-operate" with intelligence officials?*
- *Are you willing to participate in firing squads?*

Mostafa Pour-Mohammadi, a member of the 'Death Committee', was until mid-2017 former President Hassan Rouhani's Justice Minister! When his part in the murders became known publicly, he was replaced by Alireza Avaei, who himself was a prominent executioner during the 1988 massacre, in his role as Chief Prosecutor in the city of Dezful. Avaei has been on the EU's terrorist blacklist for years.[30] Other members of the 1988 Death Committee also still hold prominent positions in Iran. Former President Hassan Rouhani himself must have been aware of the massacre as he was deputy head of the Iranian military at that time.

Back in the 1980s, members and supporters of the PMOI/MEK who were not executed or imprisoned in Iran, were forced into exile, moving to Paris and other European and North American cities. Despite their political differences with Khomeini, the PMOI/MEK did everything to avoid confrontation with him and his regime.[31]

---

[29] Amnesty International, op. cit. 11

[30] Council Decision 2011/235/CFSP of 12 April 2011 concerning restrictive measures directed against certain persons and entities in view of the situation in Iran.

[31] From February 1979 to June 20, 1981, the PMOI/MEK exhibited remarkable restraint, refusing to retaliate against attacks by regime hooligans (Abrahamian, op. cit. 198). The organization expressed its commitment to peaceful forms of protest and endeavoured to reform the new state through democratic and nonviolent means.

Instead, it sought change through peaceful means. But when the PMOI/MEK had exhausted all possible paths to political participation,[32] as a measure of last resort the organization took up arms against the Iranian regime. Massoud Rajavi has said: 'The Islam that we profess does not condone bloodshed. We have never sought, nor do we welcome, confrontation and violence. If Khomeini is prepared to hold truly free elections, I will return to my homeland immediately. The Mojahedin will lay down their arms to participate in such elections. We do not fear election results, whatever they may be. Before the start of the armed struggle, we tried to utilise all legal means of political activity, but suppression compelled us to take up arms.'[33]

The PMOI/MEK during this period is best described as an armed resistance movement, fighting tyranny and oppression in their homeland.[34] What the PMOI/MEK has never been in its history (past

---

Referring to the events of 1979-81, the US State Department stated in a 1984 report that the PMOI "also entered avidly into the national debate on the structure of the new Islamic regime. The Mujahedin announced that its members would disarm to prove that they were not initiating the clashes with the fundamentalists that had become endemic during the campaign. The fundamentalists responded by once again banning Mujahedin representatives from the university campuses." See U.S. State Department, unclassified report on the Mojahedin, December 1984.

[32] The PMOI's peaceful campaign was halted by the regime's killing spree on June 20, 1981, during a peaceful demonstration in which some 500,000 people gathered in Tehran alone to support the organization. The regime's Revolutionary Guards opened fire on the demonstration, killing and wounding hundreds of civilians. (Mojahed weekly No. 127, Tehran, June 23, 1981. Also see Abrahamian, op. cit. 218-9).

[33] Massoud Rajavi, interview with L'Unité, Paris, January 1, 1984.

[34] In seminal ruling in April 2011, French Investigative Magistrate of Paris antiterrorism department issued a decision after an exhaustive 8-year investigation of the PMOI/MEK's entire dossier, which stated that the MEK's actions amounted to legitimate resistance against tyranny. It said: " The dossier does not contain any evidence indicating an armed activity that would intentionally target civilians. If such evidence were available, it would confirm terrorism and would annul any reference to resistance against tyranny, because resistance against tyranny at least requires that the tyrant, meaning the ruling regime, be targeted and not those oppressed, meaning the people." (Bloomfield, Lincoln Jr. The Ayatollahs and the MEK, University of Baltimore, 2019, p. 3).

or present) is a terrorist organisation.[35] The PMOI/MEK has never sought to achieve its goals using terror. It has never targeted civilians, nor have civilians ever been injured or killed because of PMOI/MEK campaigns against the Iranian regime. It was the unjust, illegal, and immoral terrorist designation of the PMOI/MEK first imposed by the Clinton Administration in America and then echoed in the UK and EU as an act of appeasement to the mullahs,[36] that acted as a recruiting tool for politicians from around the world who agreed to challenge the designation in successive courts of law. They were vindicated when the verdicts of courts in the United Kingdom, the United States and the European Union ruled that the PMOI/MEK was not a terrorist organization. Indeed, senior judges in the UK stated that the grounds on which the British government had agreed to designate the PMOI/MEK as a terrorist organization were 'perverse.'[37]

Forced into exile, Massoud Rajavi moved to Paris in 1981. He, along with the PMOI/MEK leadership, members, and supporters of the organisation, continued their opposition to Khomeini and his tyrannical rule from exile, while the movement's underground

---

[35] This has been corroborated by nearly 20 favourable court rulings in the US and Europe, which criticized their governments for mislabelling the PMOI/MEK as a "terrorist" organization. For example, on June 1, 2012, a three-judge panel of the U.S. Court of Appeals for the D.C. Circuit ruled that it will delist the MEK itself if the State Department fails to make a decision in four months. <http://www.cadc.uscourts.gov/internet/opinions.nsf/5A8913CA6D08CB2785257A100050A6D7/$file/12-1118-1376542.pdf>.

[36] One day after then Secretary of State Madeleine Albright designated the PMOI/MEK, a senior Clinton Administration official told the Los Angeles Times, "The inclusion of the People's Mojahedin was intended as a goodwill gesture to Tehran and its newly elected president, Mohammed Khatami." ("U.S. Designates 30 Groups as Terrorists," by Norman Kempster, Los Angeles Times, October 9, 1997). Also see The Wall Street Journal, 22 May 2006, and The Washington Times, May 28, 2003, and Newsweek on the Web, September 26, 2002.

[37] On November 30, 2007, the Proscribed Organisations Appeal Commission (POAC), annulled the British government's decision to list the MEK. POAC considered volumes of testimony and evidence, including classified evidence submitted by the British government. After months of investigation, it ruled that the listing of the MEK was not only "unlawful" but "perverse." (Clare Dyer, "Government ordered to end 'perverse' terror listing of Iran opposition," The Guardian, December 1, 2007).

network was operating in Iran. However, in 1986 the PMOI/MEK relocated to Iraq, after they came under increasing pressure from the government of Jacques Chirac to leave France. Attempting to secure the release of French hostages held by agents of the Iranian regime in Lebanon, the French Government was engaged in negotiations with the Iranian regime, a concession being the expulsion of the PMOI/MEK from French soil.[38]

Much has been made of this relocation to Iraq by the organisation's critics, who question the wisdom of the decision at a time when Iran was at war with Iraq. Mohammad Mohaddessin, Chairman of the Foreign Affairs Committee of the NCRI, has said of this move: "Although the French Government's pressures on the Iranian Resistance to leave France had been going on for over a year, Rajavi decided to move to Iraq only when he was assured of the Resistance's independence in Iraq and the non-interference of the Iraqi Government in its affairs. In return, the Resistance would not intervene in Iraq's internal affairs under any circumstances."

The Resistance's move to Iraq in 1986 was taking place at a time when regional alignments were vastly different from the situation after Iraq's invasion of Kuwait and the 1991 Gulf War. At the time, all European countries and the United States had warm relations with the Iraqi Government. With the very real spectre of the Iranian regime militarily defeating Iraq and occupying that country, Arab countries in the region and Western powers were doing their utmost to prevent such a disastrous outcome to the war, which clearly would have led to the rapid rise of Islamic fundamentalism and extremism across the Middle East and North Africa.

The PMOI/MEK was also very critical of Khomeini's attempts to create a satellite 'Islamic Republic' in Iraq, with the export of Islamic fundamentalism to Iraq and the wider Middle East. After Iraq had withdrawn from Iranian territory and stated its intention to compensate Iran for the war, the PMOI/MEK advocated peace with

---

[38] "France Ousts Rajavi, Exiled Khomeini Foe," Los Angeles Times, June 8, 1986.

Iraq and an end to the war.[39] The war should have ended in 1982, but instead it continued for a further six years until August 1988. Most of the casualties on the Iranian side occurred during this period, deaths which could have been avoided had Khomeini accepted Iraq's offer of peace in 1982. Instead, Khomeini proclaimed that he would not stop until an Islamic Republic, at the cost of over a million dead Iranians and Iraqis, replaced the government of Iraq.[40] Khomeini's slogan at the time, which summed up his ambition, was to 'liberate Jerusalem via Karbala'. According to this plan, Iran should have first captured and liberated the holy Shi'ite city of Karbala in Iraq and then moved towards Jerusalem.

The PMOI/MEK was faced with a difficult dilemma. On one hand the war continued and the PMOI leadership was fully aware that its call for peace could be misused by Khomeini to make propaganda, claiming the organisation was working with the enemy. On the other hand, hundreds of thousands of Iranians lives were at stake. Schoolchildren were being sent to clear mines.[41] The PMOI/MEK had to make a choice; either to be silent and let Khomeini send hundreds of thousands of people to their deaths, or to raise the flag of peace. Finally, it was the PMOI/MEK nationwide peace campaign, and its presence in Iraq, which broke the back of Khomeini's war-mongering policy.

---

[39] On March 13, 1983, the coalition of NCRI, which the PMOI/MEK is a member of, presented a peace plan, unanimously adopted by its members. Among other things, it underscored the need for an "immediate declaration of cease-fire," "withdrawal by both countries of their forces to the border lines as specified in the protocols on Re-demarcation of Land Borders between Iran and Iraq and the protocol on Demarcation of Iran-Iraq Water Borders and the Descriptive Minutes of the Maps and Aerial Photographs," and "exchange of all prisoners of war within a maximum period of three months after the declaration of the cease-fire." (https://apa-ice.org/wp-content/uploads/2019/07/Peace-plan-NCRI-003.pdf)

[40] In addition to the human toll, former Iranian president Ali-Akbar Hashemi-Rafsanjani said in a speech that the war left over 1,000 billion dollars in economic damages. (Friday Prayer sermon, Tehran radio, August 9, 1991).

[41] On October 31, 1997, Hashemi Rafsanjani acknowledged that about 36,000 schoolboys were sent to the warfronts. ("The Influence of Promoting the Culture of War and Martyrdom on the Morale of Children and Teenagers," Radio France Internationale (RFI), May 27, 2019.

Chapter Six

PRESIDENTS OF THE ISLAMIC REPUBLIC OF IRAN

Following the 1979 revolution and overthrow of the Shah, the first president of the Islamic Republic of Iran was **Abolhassan Banisadr**. He was a lay political activist, who had thrown his support behind Ayatollah Khomeini, believing him to be a spiritual leader who would not remain directly involved in politics. It was a grave mistake. Banisadr was elected president in 1980, while the mullahs were temporarily distracted, attempting to consolidate power by crushing other activist and nationalist groups. When a full-scale invasion of Iran by neighbouring Iraq took place on 22nd September 1980, Banisadr became the overall war commander of Iranian forces. But as tensions rose between the clerics and the non-clerical politicians, Banisadr found himself increasingly isolated and under threat from the regime. Banisadr was persuaded by the opposition PMOI/MEK to form a de facto alliance against Khomeini's reactionary clerical regime.

Figure 10 - Abolhassan Banisadr – First President of Iran

When he was impeached by the parliament in June 1981, Massoud Rajavi formed the National Council of Resistance of Iran (NCRI) while still in Tehran on July 20, 1981 and invited Banisadr to join.[42] The PMOI/MEK facilitated Banisadr's safe passage out of Iran along with Rajavi by the end of July. Banisadr lived in exile in Paris for the next forty years until his death. Iranian Air Force pilot, Colonel Behzad Moezi, one of the most prestigious Air Force officers and the former Shah's personal pilot, who joined the PMOI/MEK secretly, piloted an Iranian military plane out of Mehrabad Tactical Air Base 1, in a highly sophisticated operation to transport Mr. Rajavi to Paris. Mr. Rajavi also took Banisadr with him on the same plane to Paris, where he had lived for many years before the revolution.

Figure 11 - Mohammad-Ali Rajai was president for only 28 days.

Banisadr's brief term in office was followed by an even shorter tenure. **Mohammad-Ali Rajai** became the second president of the Islamic Republic. As a fierce anti-monarchist and one-time

---

[42] Nashriye Anjomanhaye Daneshjouyan-e Mosalman (Associations of Muslim Students Publication), No. 10, October 23, 1981.

supporter of the PMOI/MEK, he was arrested at least twice and tortured by the Shah's SAVAK secret police, spending several years in jail during the 1970s. After the 1979 revolution he became education minister then prime minister under Abolhassan Banisadr, before becoming president on 2nd August 1981. Rajai was assassinated together with prime minister Mohammad-Javad Bahonar and three others, in a bomb attack on 30th August 1981. He had been president for only 28 days.

Figure 12 - Ali Khamenei, supreme leader of theocratic regime in Iran.

Sayyid Ali Khamenei, who is currently the Islamic Republic's 2nd Supreme Leader, became the third president of Iran following Rajai's assassination. He was elected in October 1981 and was the first cleric to serve as president, remaining in post until 16 August 1989. Subjected to an intensive religious education from the age of four, he spent his basic and advanced seminary studies at the religious seminary of Mashhad. In 1958 he moved to Qom, where he became a student of Ruhollah Khomeini and began to take a keen interest in politics. In June 1981 he was seriously injured during an assassination attempt, permanently losing the use of his right arm, following the explosion of a bomb hidden in a tape recorder.

Khamenei was president during the massacre of 30,000 political prisoners in 1988 and must be held to account for that atrocity.[43]

Figure 13 - Akbar Hashemi Rafsanjani

Akbar Hashemi Rafsanjani became the fourth President of Iran on 16th August 1989 and served two terms (1989-1997). Rafsanjani was considered one of the founders of the Islamic Republic, attempting to rebuild Iran's shattered infrastructure and economy after the Iran-Iraq war. He was head of the Assembly of Experts and Chairman of the Expediency Discernment Council. His powerful position enabled him to select Ali Khamenei as Supreme Leader, following the death of Ayatollah Ruhollah Khomeini in 1989 and the dismissal of Ayatollah Montazeri.

A millionaire mullah, Rafsanjani was one of Iran's richest men, portraying himself as a moderate reformer, while in fact he exploited his political networks for personal financial gain. By 2002 he had fallen out with the hard-line clerics, and IRGC leaders and was denied a seat in parliament during a sham election. In the same

---

[43] Amnesty International

year, however, he became head of the Expediency Council and remained in that post until his death aged 82 in 2017. He ran again for the presidency in 2005, losing to Mahmoud Ahmadinejad in a heavily disputed election. He tried to run again in 2013, but was barred from standing by Iran's electoral watchdog, presumably acting on Khamenei's orders. He then became a key supporter of Hassan Rouhani.

Figure 14 - Mohammad Khatami

Mohammad Khatami became the fifth President of Iran on 3rd August 1997 and served two terms (1997-2005). Representing a defeated faction of the regime that was increasingly dominated by Ali Khamenei, Khatami styled himself as a moderate reformer, stood on a platform of freedom of expression and tolerance, and presented his vision of 'Dialogue Amongst Civilizations' as a way to make headway on Iran's international front, claiming that his strategy of dialogue with the West would win the regime more benefits than confrontation. He won 70% of the popular vote in his first election as president, with a reported voter turnout of over 80%. Khatami announced his intention to run for the 2009 presidential election, before suddenly withdrawing and throwing his support behind the former Prime Minister Mir-Hossein Mousavi, causing great consternation in elite circles of the mullahs and IRGC. Khatami repeatedly clashed with the hard-line, conservative mullahs, with his attempts at reform often being defeated by the Guardian Council on the orders of Khamenei. Khatami repeatedly backed down in facing Khamenei and never could stand up to him. In the 1999 student uprising, 24 IRGC generals, including Qassem Soleimani and Hossein Salami (the current IRGC commander) wrote to Khatami demanding he show firmness against the protesters. Khatami bowed to their demand and allowed the IRGC to suppress the protests. Ultimately, Khatami's followers became disillusioned with his lack of progress and deserted him.

Figure 15 - Holocaust denier - President Mahmud Ahmadinejad

Khatami's presidency was followed in 2005 by the election of the rank outsider **Mahmoud Ahmadinejad**. The son of a blacksmith, Ahmadinejad became a student leader during the revolution and went on to join the IRGC. He rose to become mayor of Tehran before becoming the sixth president of the Islamic Republic. A vitriolic hater of Israel and a holocaust denier, Ahmadinejad was seen as something of a joke in the West, although for the Iranian people, his two terms in office were certainly no cause for humour. His re-election in 2009 was regarded as a total sham.

One could only admire the zeal of the brave young people of Iran as they took to the streets following Ahmadinejad's faked re-election, demanding an end to the mullahs' theocratic dictatorship. Their courageous resistance against their fundamentalist rulers showed the free world that the regime does not speak for the Iranian population. No one believed the election results or the figures the regime claimed for voter turnout.[44] It was Leon Trotsky who said: "It is not the people who vote that count, but the people who count the votes." That was certainly true in this election.

The main resistance coalition, the NCRI, had undercover observers at 25,000 of the 40,000 polling stations throughout the country.[45] They reported that turnout was extremely low. Their final estimate put overall turnout at around 15%.[46] In other words, less than 8 million Iranians voted. The mullahs, on the direct instructions of Supreme Leader Ali Khamenei, (leaked the day before the elections took place), announced that over 40 million people had cast their votes, with the incumbent Mahmoud Ahmadinejad winning by a landslide (63% of the vote). Indeed, such was the farcical nature of the mullahs' efforts to rig the election, that Ahmadinejad apparently

---

[44] According to The New York Times, "Iran's most powerful oversight council announced on Monday that the number of votes recorded in 50 cities exceeded the number of eligible voters there by three million, further tarnishing a presidential election that has set off the most sustained challenge to Iran's leadership in 30 years ("Amid Crackdown, Iran Admits Voting Errors," The New York Times, June 22, 2009).

[45] "Iran election sham – 1: Vote rigging in mullahs' election," NCRI, June 12, 2009. <ncr-iran.org/en/ncri-statements/statement-iran-protest/iran-election-sham-1-vote-rigging-in-mullahs-election/>

[46] "85 percent of Iranians boycott religious dictatorship's election," NCRI, June 13, 2009. <ncr-iran.org/en/ncri-statements/statement-iran-protest/maryam-rajavi-85-percent-of-iranians-boycott-religious-dictatorships-election/>

won a huge majority even in the villages and districts of his main opponents.

The ensuing riots which saw tens of thousands of mostly young people taking to the streets in protest, led to Khamenei, in a speech at Tehran University, calling for an end to the violence, ironically saying the outcome should be from the ballot box, not on the street.[47] He said that there was an 11 million vote difference between Mahmoud Ahmadinejad and Mir Hossein Mousavi, arguing that it would have been impossible to rig 11 million votes. However, his claim was undermined by the fact that Ahmadinejad's victory was announced before many of the polling stations had even finished counting their votes!

Undeterred, Khamenei accused Western nations of starting the clamour about ballot rigging, singling out Great Britain as a country that he said was trying to create unrest in Iran. "Keep your nose out of our business," he said, "these are domestic affairs you are meddling in, and you are responsible for the allegations of vote rigging to begin with".[48]

The regime's response to the nationwide protests was to impose the usual violent crackdown, with the expulsion of foreign journalists, the suspension of mobile phone and internet networks, dawn raids on homes and universities, sporadic killings and mass arrests.[49] But on 13th June 2009, the Iranian political landscape markedly changed. The main issue was no longer the feuding between the various factions of the regime; it was now about the people of Iran versus the totality of the religious dictatorship. Millions of ordinary men and women, who suffered immensely under the mullahs, took to the streets chanting "Death to the dictator'.[50] But as always, they

---

[47] "Iran's Top Leader Dashes Hopes for a Compromise," The New York Times, June 19, 2009.

[48] Ayatollah demands end to protests," BBC, June 19, 2009.

[49] "Iran elections: mass arrests and campus raids as regime hits back," The Guardian, June 17, 2009.

[50] "Protests Flare in Tehran as Opposition Disputes Vote," The New York Times, June 13, 2009.

paid a heavy price for their courage. Dozens were killed by the regime's Basiji militia thugs.[51]

Mrs. Maryam Rajavi said the re-appointment of Ahmadinejad would result in a sharp rise in suppression of opponents of the corrupt regime, followed by widespread internal purges and factional feuding. She also warned that Ahmadinejad would redouble his efforts to acquire nuclear weapons and to export terrorism and fundamentalism, combined with further meddling in Iraq, while simultaneously inciting conflict throughout the region, exactly the scenario that subsequently unfolded.[52]

In the UK's House of Commons, Prime Minister Gordon Brown said: "I think Iran has got to listen very carefully. ... The relationship they will have and the respect they will have from the rest of the world will depend on how they respond to what are legitimate grievances that are being expressed and have to be answered. This threat now needs to be backed up with action. The EU is Iran's largest trading partner. It is disgraceful that we are paying cash into the mullahs' coffers. Britain should ask the UN Security Council to impose smart sanctions against the regime, targeting in particular, its sale of oil".

Meanwhile news filtered out of Iran that the theocratic regime had set up a special 3-man tribunal to deal with the thousands of detainees arrested during the street protests. An estimated 2,000 students and other protesters were detained during the uprising that took place following the fraudulent re-election of Ahmadinejad. Many of the detainees faced torture and execution at the hands of the tribunal as the oppressive mullah-led regime tried desperately to re-assert control. This followed demands made by mullah Ahmad

---

[51] "Hundreds may have died in Iranian clashes after poll, say human rights campaigners," The Guardian, July 16, 2009.
[52] "Exiled group says race on in Iran to build bomb," Reuters, June 13, 2009.

Khatami, who said those arrested had "waged war on God" and should face execution.[53]

It was clear that Khamenei had ordered a tribunal of executioners to oversee the punishment of the arrested protesters. Mullah Mahmoud Hashemi-Shahroudi, the notorious head of the regime's Judiciary, had set up a three-man committee consisting of Prosecutor-General mullah Ghorbanali Dorri-Najafabadi, General Inspection Organization Director Mostafa Pour-Mohammadi and First Deputy Judiciary chief Ebrahim Raisi, the so-called 'Butcher of Tehran', who later became president.

This new committee was eerily reminiscent of the "Death Committee" founded by Ayatollah Khomeini in 1988, which in the space of a few weeks ordered the execution of 30,000 political prisoners. Pour-Mohammadi and Raisi were both members of that "Death Committee".[54] Pour-Mohammadi, a former Interior Minister under Mahmoud Ahmadinejad, was at the time of the 1988 massacre, a deputy Intelligence Minister and played a central role in carrying out Khomeini's order for the massacre of political prisoners. Dorri-Najafabadi, a former Intelligence Minister, was responsible for many killings and crimes under the theocratic regime, including the serial murders of political opponents in the late 1990s which took place while he was a minister.[55] All three members of the committee committed crimes against humanity.

---

[53] "Iranian cleric says protesters wage war against God," The Washington Post, June 27, 2009.

[54] "Iran: key officials named over 1988 mass prison killings - new report," Amnesty International, December 4, 2018.

[55] "Iran's Spy Chief Quits in Wake of Dissidents'," Los Angeles Times, February 10, 1999.

Figure 16 - The wolf in sheep's clothing – President Hassan Rouhani

Internationally, Ahmadinejad, a holocaust denier who called for Israel to be "wiped off the map", was regarded as a dangerous clown. At the end of his second term, he was replaced by **Hassan Rouhani,** who served two terms as president from 2013-2021. Once again, Rouhani tried to pitch himself as a moderate reformer. Just how 'moderate' Rouhani was could be judged from the 2,400 people who were executed in Iran during his first two years in office. Under Rouhani's presidency Iran executed more people per capita than any other country in the world.[56]

Khamenei regarded Rouhani's growing international profile with deep suspicion, seeing in him a potential threat to his own hard-line leadership. Khamenei's legacy of exporting terror to Iraq, Syria, Yemen, Lebanon and Palestine and challenging Saudi Arabia for dominance in the Middle East was on the verge of breakdown, as the military cost of proxy wars escalated, and the price of oil

---

[56] "Iran Wins World Record for Most Executions Per Capita," Foreign Policy, October 7, 2015.

collapsed. There were countless demonstrations in Iran, where ordinary people protested at the rising cost of food and fuel in a faltering economy. But Khamenei, fearful of another uprising similar to the mass demonstrations that took place after the second fraudulent election of Ahmadinejad in 2009, reacted by using brute force, arbitrary arrests, imprisonment, torture and public hangings to subdue social unrest.

Rouhani's presidency was marked by the signing in Vienna in 2015 of the Joint Comprehensive Plan of Action (JCPOA) nuclear deal drawn up by Barack Obama, and the lifting of sanctions, followed subsequently by the unilateral withdrawal of the US from the agreement by President Donald Trump in 2018 and the re-imposition of tough 'maximum pressure' sanctions. Rouhani and his foreign minister Mohammad Javad Zarif, were meanwhile engaged in authorizing terrorist plots in the West, using their accredited diplomatic staff as assassins and bombers.[57]

Contrary to expectations, the JCPOA led to the regime being emboldened in its foreign interventions and terrorist attacks in Europe, which it had throttled back since 1997, but restarted again in the same year of the signing of the JCPOA.

Khamenei's disappointment with Rouhani's failures, led to his decision to manipulate the election of the 'Butcher of Tehran' as the next president of Iran, in the misguided belief that such a hard-line executioner would startle Iran's critics at home and abroad. It was another gross miscalculation.

---

[57] "Iranian Diplomat Is Convicted in Plot to Bomb Opposition Rally in France," The New York Times, February 15, 2021.

Figure 17 - Ebrahim Raisi – 'The Butcher of Tehran'

The sham election as president in 2021 of **Ebrahim Raisi**, one of the key participants in the 1988 massacre, backfired, with mass protests chanting "Death to Raisi, death to Khamenei."[58] As the leading executioner per capita in the world, it was perhaps appropriate that a notorious killer had ascended to the presidency. Listed as an international terrorist in the USA, Amnesty International[59] and Human Rights Watch[60] called for Raisi's indictment for violations of human rights and crimes against humanity.

Raisi even boasted of his role as a member of the 'Death Commission' appointed by Khomeini in 1988, which oversaw the massacre of more than 30,000 political prisoners.[61] For his work as an executioner, Raisi was promoted to the position of Tehran Prosecutor in 1989, where he earned his 'butcher' sobriquet. He held that position for five years. In 2012 he became Deputy Head of the

---

58 "Iran protests spread to major central province; unofficial death toll rises to six," Al-Arabiya, May 18, 2022.

59 "Iran: Ebrahim Raisi must be investigated for crimes against humanity," Amnesty International, June 19, 2021.

60 "Iran: Overseer of Mass Executions Elected President," Human Rights Watch, June 19, 2021.

61 "Iran's president-elect defends himself over 1988 executions," Associated Press, June 21, 2021.

Judiciary. Raisi became head of Iran's Judiciary in March 2019. Since that time, he has directed scores of executions.[62] At 27, he was the youngest of 4 members of a special 'Death Committee' for Tehran, set up by the then Supreme Leader Ayatollah Ruhollah Khomeini. Similar committees were operating in most large cities across Iran in 1988, following Khomeini's 'fatwa' against the PMOI/MEK, whom he condemned to execution for "waging war against God." Even pregnant women and teenagers were not spared.

Raisi's role as one of the key executioners was exposed during his campaign for the presidency in 2021. He brazenly implied that he should be applauded for killing thousands of Iranians when he said: "I am proud to have defended human rights in every position I have held so far. In the role of a prosecutor, wherever I may be, I am proud to defend the rights, security, and welfare of the people." Agnès Callamard, secretary general of Amnesty International, has demanded that Raisi be investigated for "crimes against humanity" by the U.N. Human Rights Council. "The circumstances surrounding the fate of the victims and the whereabouts of their bodies are, to this day, systematically concealed by the Iranian authorities," Callamard said.[63]

Raisi has been subject to sanctions by Washington since 2019 for 'complicity in serious human rights violations.'[64] Since being manoeuvred into the presidency in a sham election in August 2021, the number of executions in Iran skyrocketed. A year into his presidency, by August 2022, at least 521 prisoners had been

[62] "Raisi accused of using position at judiciary for mass executions," AFP, June 16, 2021.

[63] "Iran: Ebrahim Raisi must be investigated for crimes against humanity," Amnesty International, June 19, 2021.

[64] "Treasury Designates Supreme Leader of Iran's Inner Circle Responsible for Advancing Regime's Domestic and Foreign Oppression," U.S. Department of the Treasury, November 4, 2019.

executed, including 22 women and six minors.[65] 71 people were hanged in July 2022 alone, two of them in public. Several medieval sentences were also handed down, including a woman and two men who were sentenced to be blinded. Their sentences were upheld by Iran's Supreme Court. Even teenagers convicted of theft in juvenile courts were sentenced to have their fingers amputated. Raisi's term in office was saturated with blood and repression. There is no doubt that his reputation as a ruthless slaughterer was one of the principal reasons he was chosen as the preferred candidate for the presidency by Supreme Leader Ali Khamenei. At least 100 prisoners have died in prison, while least 18,144 people have been arrested and 2,000 detained for political reasons, under Raisi's presidency.[66] There have also been five cases of flogging and two cases of amputation of limbs during the summer of 2022. The recent crackdown on women intensified their suppression in the framework of the medieval decree passed by Raisi's government entitled 'chastity and hijab,' enforcing a draconian dress code.

---

[65] Stevenson, Struan, "Iran's blood-soaked president, Ebrahim Raisi, must be banned from United Nations' General Assembly – Struan Stevenson," The Scotsman, August 26, 2022.

[66] 2022. "Iran: Ebrahim Raisi's Presidency, One Year On - NCRI." Ncr-iran. August 3, 2022. https://www.ncr-iran.org/en/news/iran-resistance/iran-ebrahim-raisis-presidency-one-year-on/.

Chapter Seven

UNMASKING THE MONARCHISTS

The first group of Iranians that left Iran after the 1979 revolution was a diverse range of monarchists who harboured hopes of one day returning to their homeland. They enjoyed wide support from the US, Saudi Arabia, Turkey, and Egypt. In the first few years, some of the Shah's generals announced the formation of a fighting force composed of the Shah's military officers in Turkey and on the Iranian border. They had vast financial support. But the ruse was soon exposed as a publicity stunt and such activities ground to a complete stop by 1984.

Over the past four decades, numerous groups have formed, then been dissolved, or disintegrated under the banner of Iranian monarchism. Despite the apparent existence of abundant financial resources, and despite their mass exodus from Iran in 1979, monarchist groups were never able to transform themselves into a viable political force. There are many reasons for this dysfunction. On the one hand, the monarchy was irrefutably rejected by most Iranian people. Their time had come and gone in Iran. On the other hand, widespread corruption among the leaders of the monarchists, on top of their daily political bickering, led to deep divisions among their number. Despite this, monarchist elements have maintained commercial and cultural dealings with Iran under the mullahs, and the regime has used this opportunity widely and deeply to infiltrate their ranks and steer them in line with their own objectives.

Although there are some in Iran who may still believe in the monarchist system, yet there is no monarchist political group inside Iran. The overwhelming majority of those who were alive during the revolution of 1979 have rejected the monarchy. There is no indication that the new generation has any tendency or wish to restore the monarchy in Iran. The most important indicator of the lack of support for the monarchist movement was the January 2018, and specifically the November 2019 uprisings, in which the Iranian people completely rejected Reza Pahlavi's proposal for civil disobedience and cooperation with the IRGC.[67] Isolated publicity stunts claiming support for the monarchy, that were mounted by agents of the regime to distort the demands of the demonstrators, backfired, failing to provide any credibility to the monarchists. It did, however, expose how the regime plays the monarchist card.

Figure 18 - Reza Pahlavi – self-proclaimed Crown Prince of Iran.

In 1980, after his father's death, Reza Pahlavi proclaimed himself Reza Shah II, and said he wanted to have a constitutional monarchy like the King of Spain. Despite claiming that he wanted the Iranian people to have the freedom to choose if they wanted to restore him as King, he nevertheless proclaimed himself Shah or King while in

---

[67] While the IRGC plays a central role in suppressing protesters on the streets, Reza Pahlavi has routinely supported the IRGC's "rank-and-file." In December 2018, he told a think tank in Washington: "People have to send signals to the Basijis and the Pasdars [IRGC], and vice versa. That we can stand together as opposed to continue being versus each other" (Interview with The Washington Institute for Near East Policy, December 18, 2018).

Egypt, although even some monarchists are opposed to him as their next Shah. But once more, despite abundant financial resources, he has never been able to assemble supporters of the monarchy in exile and form a cohesive group or organization during the past four decades, underlining the fact that the monarchy is a spent force that belongs to the past and has nothing to offer for the future of Iran.

For several years Reza Pahlavi was the spokesperson for an organization known as the National Council of Iran, announcing its formation in an interview he gave on March 7, 2013. How the council was formed is also quite revealing. In late 2009 and early 2010 three former diplomats of the Iranian regime left their posts to join the green movement abroad. The three individuals were members of the coordinating committee of what they called the 'Green Movement of Hope', and formed a new group called the 'Green Embassy Campaign.' One of the founders of the 'Green Movement of Hope' was none other than Ayatollah Hashemi Rafsanjani, one of the primary aides and advisors to the regime's founder and Supreme Leader, Ayatollah Ruhollah Khomeini.

In the second half of 2011, the 'Green Embassy Campaign' proposed the formation of an alternative political party. Ali Akbar Amirmehr, one of the three founding members of the 'Green Embassy Campaign', recounted how they had contacted a wide range of opposition groups that stood for overthrowing the regime, asking for solidarity, but that those groups did not welcome the call. Reza Pahlavi, on the other hand, was the first person to support them. In an interview on Monday, September 10, 2012, Amirmehr said: "We contacted leaders of Democratic Seculars, Green Wave, National Front, National Religionists seeking dissolution of the regime, Constitutional Monarchists, Republicans, independent and national and non-affiliated leftists, who all sought overthrow and not reform, and we humbly invited them to unite with us. Perhaps you would be surprised to know that the first person who welcomed our call was Reza Pahlavi..."

It became clear that the theocratic regime had penetrated the monarchists' National Council of Iran movement and even helped

Reza Pahlavi in the preparation of its charter, in the final version of which there is no article that demands the overthrow, elimination, or change of the velayat-e faqih regime. Some monarchists condemned Reza Pahlavi's involvement with this group and warned him that, as in the past, he had been duped by the mullahs' Ministry of Intelligence (MOIS).

It appeared from statements he made during the 2018 and 2019 nationwide uprisings in Iran, that Reza Pahlavi believes he can achieve regime change by cooperation with the IRGC and the Basij paramilitary force! He claims that he is in contact with some elements within the Revolutionary Guards and the Basij, asserting that even after the overthrow of the regime the same forces will be guarantors of the peaceful transition of power. It therefore appears that by his own admission, Reza Pahlavi is associated with elements within the IRGC and the Basij.

The monarchy in Iran was an illegitimate and autocratic institution that a popular revolution overthrew. The notion of the return of the monarchy to Iran is as historically anachronistic as the return of the monarchy to France or Russia, or even Iraq and Afghanistan. Such a fantasy is irrelevant and does not merit serious consideration.

The Iranian regime plays up the monarchy card as a ploy to maintain its clerical rule and deprive the Iranian people of their right to self-rule and sovereignty. The monarchists are also touted from time to time by Western political circles detached from the reality of Iran. Former members of SAVAK, who migrated to the US and UK and other countries after the revolution, joined the intelligence services of their newly adopted countries. But as they rose through the ranks, these new members of the Western intelligence communities, skewed professional intelligence analysis of the events in Iran based on an inclination of restoring a rejected monarchy, and agitated against genuine, homegrown democratic forces such as the PMOI/MEK.

Iranian monarchists do not have any grassroots organizational capability in either Iran or anywhere else. During the past 40 years, monarchists have not played any role or paid any price in fighting the regime. Reza Pahlavi has no concrete plans for regime change other than talking up a fantasy of cooperation with the regime's repressive forces like the IRGC and Basij. He has no plans for the future of Iran. Even his official website does not purport to have a program for the future of Iran.

Chapter Eight

NATIONAL COUNCIL OF RESISTANCE OF IRAN (NCRI)

The PMOI/MEK is one of five member organisations of the National Council of Resistance of Iran, a coalition of democratic Iranian opposition groups and prominent individuals, established by Massoud Rajavi in 1981 while he was in Tehran, to oppose the theocratic regime of Ayatollah Khomeini. In exile and headquartered in Paris, it is a political coalition and parliament in-exile of about 460 members, representing all religious and ethnic minorities in Iran, including Kurds, Baluchis, Armenians, Jews, and Zoroastrians. The PMOI/MEK was headquartered in Camp Ashraf and Camp Liberty in Iraq, and now in Ashraf 3 in Albania with approximately 3,000 members. The coalition has tens of thousands of active supporters worldwide, and at least 5,000 resistance units inside Iran, without mention of its popular roots which are difficult to gauge in Iran's closed system, but one that comprises thousands of family members, supporters, and backers who actively lead its campaigns for resistance and overthrow of the regime inside the country.[68]

The NCRI is comprised of 25 committees that act as shadow ministries and are responsible for expert research and planning for a future Iran. Fifty percent of the NCRI's members are women, and a charismatic woman leads the entire coalition. Maryam Rajavi is the President-elect of the NCRI. The NCRI have representative offices throughout the world and function as a parliament-in-exile. They have country representatives and staff in each country, dedicated to informing politicians and the public on issues

---

[68] "Iran: The Nationwide Uprising and the Role of MEK Resistance Units," NCRI, September 26, 2022.

pertaining to Iran and the Middle East. As the organisation is comprised of experts in numerous fields, NCRI members and officials are often invited to provide comment on Iran, as their information and evidence is second to none. For example, it was the NCRI who first exposed the Iranian regime's nuclear weapons program by announcing the existence of a uranium enrichment facility in Natanz in 2002.[69] These revelations were based on information provided to the NCRI by the PMOI/MEK's network inside Iran, often at great personal risk.

The American government, who had no love for the Iranian resistance in 2002, confirmed the role of the PMOI/MEK in this, although they were careful not to mention the organization by name, stating: 'Iran admitted the existence of these facilities only after it had no choice, because they had been made public by an Iranian opposition group.'[70] 'Iran has concealed its nuclear program. That became discovered, not because of their compliance with the IAEA or NPT, but because a dissident group pointed it out to the world, which raised suspicions about the intentions of the program.'[71]

'An Iranian opposition group said today that it had evidence of two previously undisclosed uranium enrichment facilities west of Tehran. The group, the National Council of Resistance of Iran, an umbrella for Iranian opposition organizations, said the facilities were discovered by the People`s Mojahedin, a resistance group that brought the Natanz plant to the attention of international weapons inspectors. "This organization has been extremely on the mark in the past," said a senior United Nations official who is familiar with the situation in Iran, adding, "They are a group that seems to be privy to very solid and insider information."'[72]

---

[69] "Chronology of Iran's Nuclear Program," The New York Times, August 8, 2005.
[70] White House briefing, White House spokesman, March 10, 2003.
[71] White House Press Conference, 16 March 2005.
[72] "Group Says Iran Has 2 Undisclosed Nuclear Laboratories," The New York Times, May 27, 2003.

The NCRI organises symposiums, press conferences and exhibitions and are responsible for excellent and well-informed publications. They work tirelessly to assist the Iranian people to realise their inalienable rights to freedom, democracy and respect for human rights and fundamental freedoms. Their offices are also interestingly one of the first ports of call for Iranians who manage to escape the clutches of the Ayatollahs in Iran. They view the organisation as the embodiment of their hopes and desires for a free, democratic, and secular Iran.

Encouraged, influenced, and guided by the example set by Maryam Rajavi, the women within the PMOI are immensely capable. In the internal elections usually held every two years, PMOI members have repeatedly elected women to be their Secretary General over the past 30 years. Having been held back for decades by a misogynist regime that despises females, the women within the PMOI are a hugely influential and powerful force, representing a source of inspiration and empowerment to the millions of women in Iran. It is this fact that petrifies the Iranian regime and the reason why they have such utter contempt for the organisation and for the women within the organisation.

Figure 19 - Mrs Maryam Rajavi – President-elect of the NCRI

The role of women in Iran is extremely important, because they have been treated as second-class citizens by the mullahs for more than four decades. If we wish any further evidence of the misogynist lunacy of the clerical regime, then we should look no further than the news that Khamenei ordered that cartoon character women must wear the hijab. Now, in Iran, even animated female characters in cartoons cannot reveal their hair! It would be amusing if it wasn't so serious. Women's dress codes are under constant scrutiny. They must wear the hijab and 'morality police' are on relentless patrol to enforce the law. Women, particularly young women, are singled out for brutal attacks for the 'crime' of mal veiling. Girls who were deemed to be improperly dressed in the street have suffered horrific acid attacks and stabbings, in assaults openly condoned by the mullahs. Teenage girls, arrested for the offence of posting videos of themselves dancing or singing on social media, have been publicly flogged. Young female students attending end-of-term parties have been fined and beaten. This is what gender equality looks like in Iran today.

The toll of women executed in Iran's medieval prisons continues to rise. Most of these women were executed for killing an abusive husband or partner. But this is another example of how the regime fails women, because they are mostly victims of domestic abuse who kill in defence of themselves or their children, because they have no legal recourse to end a violently cruel marriage. These killings often occur after women have suffered years of humiliation, insults, beatings and even torture, by abusive husbands, from whom they have no escape…no right to divorce. In other countries, they would be granted leniency based on their circumstances, but not in Iran. And this, of course, does not even touch upon those executed for crimes that are not capital offences under international law, like drug offences, or for non-crimes, like political activism.

Iran is now the world leader in executions per capita, as well as executions of women and juvenile offenders.[73] Over 4,500 people have been executed since 2013, with the number of overall executions and those of women is actually believed to be much higher because of the fact that most executions take place in secret, without witnesses.[74] There are approximately 40 million women in the Islamic Republic of Iran, over half under the age of thirty. Women make up more than 50% of university students, but, because of discrimination and blatant sexism creating obstacles to employment, they accounted for only 19% of Iran's workforce. At a time when women in the West have achieved political, economic, personal and social equality, Iranian women are amongst the most repressed in the world, ruled by a regime dominated by elderly, bearded misogynists.

But young Iranian women are becoming increasingly engaged in the growing opposition to the mullahs' corrupt regime. They are joining the resistance units that are springing up in every town and city in Iran. In the nationwide uprisings that have taken place, tens of thousands of courageous female teachers, medical staff, nurses, students, factory workers and pensioners have taken to the streets to demand an end to corruption, an end to discrimination and repression and an end to the clerical regime's aggressive military adventurism across the Middle East. Hundreds of women have been amongst those killed by the IRGC and thousands more have been arrested.

In the theocratic fascist dictatorship, the Iranian penal code is designed to enable men to discipline women and girls if they fail to conform to strict Islamic codes. The theocratic dictatorship in Iran has a history of targeting women with oppressive laws that would not be tolerated in the West or indeed in most civilized countries in the world. In Iran women are considered the property of their closest male relative and have no legal rights. Girls of nine can be

---

[73] "Iran: The last executioner of children," Amnesty International, June 2007.

[74] "Iran: Horrific wave of executions must be stopped," Amnesty International, June 27, 2022.

married off by their parents. A woman's evidence in court is worth only half that of a man. Women may not seek to have a man charged with rape unless they have four independent witnesses. All family relationships are strictly controlled by Sharia law. Homosexual behaviour, adultery, sex outside marriage, are met with inhuman and cruel punishment and even execution by hanging. Women accused of such behaviour can incur severe punishments, including beatings and death, sometimes by stoning.

Ayatollah Ruhollah Khomeini, the first Supreme Leader of Iran after the 1979 revolution and the father of Islamic fundamentalism, stated that equality between women and men was "in fundamental violation of some of the most crucial rulings of Islam and in defiance of some of the explicit commandments of the Quran". Immediately following the revolution, Khomeini abolished the 'Family Protection Law' that gave women family rights. He also cancelled social services for women and abolished the role of female judges in Iran's justice system. Today, only a tiny minority of MPs in Iran are women.

Today, Iranian women are at the forefront of the resistance to the theocratic dictatorship. Indeed, the main democratic opposition movement, the PMOI/MEK is led by women. Brave women are now routinely joining their brothers to demand regime change and an end to the misogyny and repression which has terrorized not only the Iranian people for the past four decades, but a vast part of the Middle East as well.

Addressing an International Women's Day conference, Malala Yousafzai said: "We realize the importance of our voice when we are silenced." Well, the women of Iran are no longer prepared to be silenced. They will be heard and their cry for freedom and democracy, led by Maryam Rajavi, will resonate around the world.

Chapter Nine

THE EXPORT OF TERROR

One of the most horrifying consequences of the inception of the Islamic Republic of Iran in 1979 has been the export of terror and the aggressive export of Islamic fundamentalism. The PMOI/MEK, as the oldest and largest anti-fundamentalist Muslim group in the Middle East, has been invaluable to the international community in the fight against Islamic fundamentalism, now a real global threat to peace and security. Because they advocate a democratic and tolerant Islam, many Middle East experts and political figures in Europe and North America see the organisation as the antithesis to Islamic fundamentalism. The PMOI/MEK's modern, democratic, tolerant, and progressive interpretation of Islam is the opposite to what fundamentalist Islam represents. The PMOI/MEK stands for a secular system of government with complete separation of religion and state. In fact, for nearly 50 years, they have sought free and fair elections. The PMOI/MEK has always maintained that the ballot box is the only legitimate basis for government, in contrast to the fundamentalists, who believe they are ordained by God.

What is particularly dangerous about the Iranian regime is their policy of expansionist ideology. Not content with inflicting indescribable misery on the Iranian people, they have exported their Islamic fundamentalism to Iraq, Syria, Yemen, Lebanon and beyond. The IRGC and their ruthless Quds Force responsible for extra-territorial operations, was formed by Ayatollah Khomeini shortly after he hijacked the 1979 revolution and seized power. Before the Iran-Iraq war, various units of the IRGC expended a lot of resources interfering in neighbouring countries to export terrorism and fundamentalism. After the war, IRGC units involved in such operations were consolidated in the Quds Force (under the IRGC command). The Iranian Resistance revealed the existence of the Quds Force in the book "Islamic Fundamentalism: The New

Global Threat" in 1992.[75] The formation of the Quds Force and pursuing a nuclear weapons programme are flip sides of the same coin, a unified strategy of the religious fascist regime ruling Iran. The regime's leaders have always touted asynchronous warfare in their perceived crusade against the West.

Khamenei tasked the IRGC and Quds Force with defending the regime's twisted fundamentalist dogmas. They became the guardians of the revolution, responsible for exporting Islamic fundamentalism worldwide.

Answerable only to the supreme leader, the IRGC controls around 50% of the Iranian economy.[76] They pay no tax. Venal corruption has enriched their commanders, who drive expensive cars and live in lavish villas, while ordinary Iranians starve. They groom, train and finance Iran's proxies in Syria, Yemen, Iraq, Lebanon, the Palestinian territories, and even in Somalia and Nigeria, causing bloodshed and conflict wherever they operate. Their revered commander, until he was killed by a drone-strike at Baghdad Airport ordered by President Trump in January 2020, was the infamous General Qassem Soleimani, a listed terrorist responsible for thousands of innocent deaths, including hundreds of Americans. Indeed, it was Trump who listed the IRGC as a Foreign Terrorist Organization in 2019, in an unprecedented step designating an integral part of another government as an FTO.

When it comes to the export of terrorism, the IRGC and the Quds Force are not the regime's only instruments of implementing its terrorist plots. The Ministry of Intelligence and Security (MOIS) also plays an important and integral role in the planning and execution of such terrorist plots abroad, particularly in Europe.

The trial in Belgium of an Iranian diplomat for attempting to bomb a mass rally of Iranian opposition supporters at Villepinte near Paris

---

[75] Mohaddessin, Mohammad. 1992. "Islamic Fundamentalism: The New Global Threat: Roundhouse Publishing Ltd: Mohaddessin, Mohammad: 9780929765228: Books.".

[76] "Showing who's boss," The Economist, August 27, 2009.

in 2018, has provided the clearest sign yet that decades of appeasement by the EU did nothing to tame this terrorist regime. Assadollah Assadi was a senior agent of the Iranian regime's sinister Ministry of Intelligence and Security (MOIS). He was using the cover of being a diplomat in the Iranian embassy in Vienna to enable him to plan a terrorist bomb attack that would have caused carnage on European soil, potentially killing hundreds of men, women and children.[77] Evidence from the Belgian prosecutor showed how Assadi had allegedly brought the professionally assembled 550 gm TATP bomb on a commercial flight to Vienna from Tehran in his diplomatic pouch and passed it, together with an envelope containing €22,000, to two co-conspirators.[78] The court was told that Assadi had instructed them how to prime and detonate the device. A third co-conspirator was posted at the Villepinte rally as a lookout. All four have now been sentenced to long terms of imprisonment.[79]

Figure 20 - Assadollah Assadi – the Iranian 'diplomat' terrorist

---

[77] Conradi, Peter. "A hellish Pizza Hut delivery: 'Iran's bomb' to take out foes in Paris," The Sunday Times, November 15, 2020.
[78] Boffey, Daniel. "Belgian court sentences Iranian diplomat to 20 years over bomb plot," The Guardian, February 4, 2021.
[79] "In first for Europe, Iran envoy sentenced to 20 -year prison term over bomb plot," Reuters, February 4, 2021.

There is no doubt Assadi's terrorist plot was ordered from the highest echelons of the regime, including the Supreme Leader Ayatollah Ali Khamenei, the president at that time Hassan Rouhani and the then foreign Minister Javad Zarif. The EU should have demanded they be held to account. So far, there has been muted criticism of this outrage from the European External Action Service (EEAS), which handles EU foreign affairs. Indeed, Europe's top diplomat, the high representative for foreign affairs and security Josep Borrell, has typically said little. We shouldn't be surprised. The first country that Borrell visited within days of taking office in December 2019 was Iran, where he met the then President Rouhani and foreign minister Zarif. Borrell pledged to "preserve" the deeply flawed nuclear deal which President Trump had unilaterally withdrawn America from, promising that Iran would "benefit economically from sanctions lifting."[80]

Figure 21 - The arch appeaser Josep Borrell meeting Iran's Foreign Minister Javad Zarif in Tehran

[80] "Press release following High Representative/Vice-President Josep Borrell's official visit to Iran," European Union External Action, February 4, 2020.

It was the same old EU refrain. Not a mention of the rampant human rights abuse and escalating number of executions taking place inside the repressive regime. Not a mention of their warmongering in Syria, Yemen, Iraq and Lebanon. Not a mention of the massacre of over 30,000 political prisoners in 1988, now the subject of a UN special inquiry. Not a mention of the 1,500 unarmed protesters who had been gunned down just weeks earlier by the Islamic Revolutionary Guards Corps (IRGC),[81] the regime's Gestapo, in the nationwide uprising which had erupted in every town and city in Iran in November 2019. The promise of an end to sanctions, so that EU businesses could re-open trade with the theocratic regime, was the message conveyed by Borrell. His signal to the mullahs was clear; for the EU, trade matters, while human rights don't.

Figure 22 - IRGC – the theocratic regime's Gestapo

Borrell may be a new singer, but this is an old song. From 1999 to 2009, Javier Solana, another Spanish socialist, was occupying the

[81] "Special Report: Iran's leader ordered crackdown on unrest - 'Do whatever it takes to end it'," Reuters, December 23, 2019.

EU's top diplomatic role. At a press conference in Washington in 2002, the NCRI revealed the existence of the Iranian regime's top-secret nuclear programme. Western intelligence agencies were caught by surprise and governments around the world were stunned. Solana was sent to Tehran to negotiate with the mullahs, offering them a package of incentives in exchange for a reduction in their uranium enrichment programme. But when the mullahs heard that Maryam Rajavi had been invited to address a meeting in the European Parliament, they threatened to boycott talks with Solana. He frantically telephoned prime ministers and presidents around the EU urging them to stop Mrs Rajavi's visit. Learning that she could be blamed for undermining Solana's negotiations, Mrs Rajavi voluntarily withdrew from her proposed meeting, but warned that the mullahs were bluffing and that they couldn't be trusted. She was right. The theocratic regime thumbed its nose at the west's compromise offers, forcing Solana, in a speech to the European Parliament, to concede that "There has been no progress. Iran continues to ignore us."

Solana's disastrous term in office was followed by two further equally ignominious high representatives. Baroness Catherine Ashton was nominated by Tony Blair and held the post from 2009 to 2014. She was succeeded by the Italian socialist Federica Mogherini, who wore the headscarf when visiting Tehran and posed for selfies with the mullahs. Both reinforced the EU's failed policy of appeasement. In doing so they sent a catastrophically wrong signal to Tehran. By offering concession after concession, the West played into the mullahs' hands, emboldening the clerics to continue their path of defiance and terror.

The trial of the Iranian diplomat Assadollah Assadi was simply the tip of a massive terrorist iceberg. The theocratic regime has used its embassies as terror cells and bomb factories for decades, perpetrating bomb attacks, murders, and kidnappings around the world. The mullahs have a history of deploying their assassins in the guise of diplomats and using their embassies around the world as terrorist hubs.

In March 2018 a terrorist plot to bomb an Iranian New Year gathering in the PMOI/MEK's settlement near Tirana was foiled. In addition to Mrs. Rajavi, several prestigious American and European dignitaries, including Rudy Giuliani, the former mayor of New York city and the personal attorney for the serving President of the United States at the time, were present.

In December 2018 the Albanian Prime Minister Edi Rama expelled the Iranian Ambassador and his First Secretary on the grounds of their involvement in the March 2018 plot. Once again these 'so-called' diplomats were revealed as trained Ministry of Intelligence and Security (MOIS) agents who had been plotting bomb attacks and assassinations of opponents of the regime in Albania.

Later in October 2019, the Albanian Police announced further details related to this case and stated that the Quds Force had hired criminal gangs in Turkey and the Balkans to carry out the above terrorist plot with intelligence provided by a "former member of the Mojahedin".

The Albanian government severed diplomatic relations and closed the Iranian regime's embassy in September 2022 because of these hostile acts in support of terrorism on Albanian soil.

Revelations by the US government in the summer of 2022 that the Iranian regime had plotted to assassinate President Trump's national security adviser – John Bolton, demonstrated once again how the Islamic Republic is like a dangerous, wounded animal, lashing out to preserve its existence. Shahram Poursafi, an agent of the IRGC, was offered $300,000 to "eliminate" Bolton. Poursafi is still at large. Assistant Attorney General Matthew Olsen, from the US Department of Justice's national security division, said: "This is not the first time we have uncovered Iranian plots to exact revenge against individuals on US soil and we will work tirelessly to expose and disrupt every one of these efforts." It is thought that Tehran ordered the murder of Bolton in revenge for the drone attack in January 2020 which killed the IRGC terrorist general Qassem Soleimani at Baghdad Airport.

The arch criminal is Ayatollah Ali Khamenei. There can be no doubt that he, together with his senior ministers, ordered the espionage, the bomb plots and the assassinations. Khamenei is praying that President Joe Biden will quickly restore Barack Obama's deeply flawed 'Joint Comprehensive Plan of Action' (JCPOA), the nuclear deal that was unceremoniously dumped by Donald Trump. He is praying that Joe Biden will lift the sanctions which prevented Iran from selling oil, crippling its economy. Biden has repeatedly confirmed that this is one of his foreign policy priorities. It would be a grave mistake. President Biden need not think that lifting sanctions would put food back on the table for impoverished Iranians. In fact, it would enable Khamenei to reinforce his funding of Bashar al-Assad's bloody civil war in Syria, the Houthi rebels in Yemen, the brutal Shi'a militias in Iraq and the terrorist Hezbollah in Lebanon. It would also enable the mullahs to accelerate their development of a nuclear weapon and ballistic missile delivery systems, which have never ceased.

When in February 2021, US Secretary of State Antony Blinken decided to take the Iranian-backed Houthi rebels in Yemen off America's terrorist blacklist, it was supposed to mark a new humanitarian approach by the Biden administration. It was a serious mistake. Blinken explained that the dire situation in Yemen, including access to basic commodities like food and fuel, had been exacerbated by US sanctions and blacklisting the Houthis. He claimed he wanted to alleviate the suffering of people affected by what he described as one of the world's worst humanitarian crises.

The Houthi rebels have been at war with the internationally recognised government of President Abd Rabbu Mansour Hadi since 2014. They quickly gained control of large tracts of Yemen, including the capital city Sanaa. In March 2015, Saudi Arabia joined the fight, initiating an air campaign against the Iranian-backed rebels, who have retaliated by launching missile and drone attacks against Saudi oil installations and population centres, as well as towns and cities in the UAE, after they joined the Arab coalition against the Houthis. It has become a bloody conflict. With American logistical support there have been more than 18,000 Arab coalition raids on Houthi-held positions. Over 130,000 people have been killed in the fighting and millions have been impoverished and displaced. Yemen, already one of the poorest countries in the Middle East, has been pushed to the brink of starvation. But, despite the ferocious air raids on Houthi positions, ammunition dumps and bases, little progress has so far been made towards re-capturing Sanaa.

The Samad-3 type suicide-drones used in the attack on Abu Dhabi international airport in January 2022, killed 3 people at the state-owned oil company ADNOC. They were supplied by the Iranian regime. Further drone and missile attacks targeting the UAE continued in 2022, provoking a call for the Shi'ite Houthi militants to be re-listed as international terrorists. The Saudis have launched a series of retaliatory airstrikes on Houthi-held parts of Yemen, including Sanaa, killing scores of civilians and temporarily shutting down the Yemeni internet. The escalating conflict has been funded and supplied by the fundamentalist theocratic Iranian regime, whose policy of aggressive expansionism across the Middle East has seen them pour billions into proxy wars in the zone, despite 80% of the Iranian population struggling to survive on daily incomes below the international poverty line. Iran's mullahs have backed Bashar al-Assad's civil war in Syria for 12 years and they continue to finance and direct the Shi'a militias in Iraq, Hezbollah in Lebanon and Hamas in Gaza.

Lurching from crisis to crisis as their economy crumbles and daily protests erupt across the country, the Iranian mullahs have nevertheless continued to invest heavily in military drone production. The theocratic regime regard unmanned aerial vehicles (UAV's) as a primary tool of their Islamic Revolutionary Guards Corps' (IRGC's) extra-territorial Quds Force. They have used drones for targeted attacks on oil tankers in international waters in the Gulf of Oman. On 29th July 2021, two drones were launched at a Liberian-flagged oil tanker with Israeli connections, as it sailed off the coast of Oman. Both drones missed their target and landed in the ocean. However, the following day, July 30th, 2021, a drone, heavily armed with "military grade" explosives, hit the tanker, blasting a six-foot hole in the ship and killing a Romanian and a British crewman. Houthi fighters in Yemen use civilian facilities at Sanaa airport and the Red Sea port of Hodeidah as bases to launch ballistic missiles and drones. Since Vladimir Putin launched his illegal invasion of Ukraine, the mullahs' regime has supplied thousands of kamikaze drones to the Russians, which they use to target Ukrainian civilian power stations and other infrastructure.

Intelligence reports from resistance units inside the theocratic regime also indicate that mercenaries and militants from dozens of terrorist organizations supported by the mullahs, regularly travel to Iran for advanced UAV training by the Quds Force, including on the use of missiles and sabotage operations. Pre-assembled drones are then despatched to target countries through the IRGC's base at Mehrabad International Airport in Tehran, or sent clandestinely by truck to Syria, Iraq, Lebanon and Palestine, hidden in containers, or sometimes by sea to Yemen and other areas.

In May 2021, the guided-missile cruiser USS Monterey, announced that it had intercepted and seized a shipment of thousands of assault weapons, machine guns, sniper rifles, anti-tank guided missiles and ammunition, hidden on board a ship in the Arabian Sea, heading to Yemen from Iran. The weapons were clearly for the Houthi rebels. The ship, after being cleared of weapons, was later released by the US. But shortly afterwards, the same vessel was once again stopped in the Gulf of Oman by the US Navy and found to be carrying 40 tons of explosive material used for making IED's (improvised explosive devices). Once again it was bound for Yemen from Iran.

Yemeni Prime Minister Maeen Abdul Malik Saeed told journalists in the Middle East that recent discussions in Washington showed that the Biden administration had "belatedly" concluded that the de-listing of the Houthis had been counterproductive. He said that since they had been removed from the US global terrorist list, the Houthis had increased their deadly strikes inside and outside Yemen, claiming many civilian lives. He said they had undermined international maritime security through the Red Sea by planting water-borne explosive devices and launching attacks on ships and he called for their re-designation as global terrorists.

A spokesperson in the UAE embassy in Yemen stated "This designation will help disrupt illicit financial and weapons networks feeding the Houthi terror machine. It will add to mounting pressure on the Houthis to engage in UN-led peace efforts that can end hostilities in a war that has gone on far too long." What is abundantly clear is that the time has come for the West to strike at the head of the Iranian octopus in Tehran, as Israel's former Prime Minister Naftali Bennett said, rather than struggling to deal with its tentacles in Syria, Iraq, Yemen, Lebanon and Gaza.

It is time for a complete change of direction in US, EU, and UN policy towards Iran. The people of Iran expect the West to be on their side. They expect their calls for democracy to be taken seriously. The appeasement policy, lamely followed by the EU, is dead in the water. Any country that seeks to use terror as statecraft should be debarred from civilized assemblies and held to account in the international courts of justice, their leaders indicted for crimes against humanity.

The mullahs also converted neighbouring Iraq into a virtual province of Iran. Many Iraqis claimed that former Prime Minister Nouri al-Maliki was worse than Saddam Hussein and that he had turned Iraq into a dust bowl of violence and bloodshed, waging a genocidal campaign against his own Sunni population and fanning the flames of a sectarian civil war. The many ethnic groups who for generations lived in peaceful harmony side-by-side with the majority Shi'a population, were now suffering systematic abuse, despite being guaranteed safety and security in a multi-faith society enshrined by the Iraqi Constitution. Maliki had become a puppet of Iran and its hard-line mullahs, pursuing a sectarian agenda outlined by Tehran, ruthlessly removing all Sunni politicians from influential government positions and cracking down hard on dissent. The predictable Sunni backlash unleashed a storm of violence that ISIS was quick to exploit.

Figure 23 - Nouri al-Maliki, the brutal dictator of Iraq

To this day, Iraq is teetering on the brink of becoming a failed state. Under Maliki, billions of dollars in oil wealth simply disappeared into illicit bank accounts. It is estimated that $550 billion in oil revenues poured into Iraq since 2006, but it simply vanished. Infrastructure projects lie dormant. Baghdad, often suffering summer heatwaves of 52 degrees centigrade, has only 4 hours of electricity a day. Few people in Iraq have access to proper functioning sewerage systems or fresh, running water. The money has simply been stolen from the people. Transparency International now lists Iraq as the 6th most corrupt country in the world. Only Somalia, Afghanistan, Sudan, South Sudan, and North Korea are worse.

In a country that won prizes for education under Saddam Hussein there is now 60% illiteracy. Unemployment is running at over 14% and with more than half the population under the age of 30, many young Iraqis are attracted to join the Shi'ite militias where they can earn $200 a week paid by Iran's Revolutionary Guards Corps (IRGC). State-condoned torture and mass executions are now commonplace.

In fact, Maliki created the perfect conditions for ISIS to enter Iraq from Syria in 2014, quickly capturing up to a third of Iraqi territory. Often the Sunni tribesmen preferred the IS jihadists to the marauding Iranian-led Shi'ite militias, who had raped, tortured, brutalized, and murdered thousands of Sunni men, women and children in Fallujah, Ramadi, Tikrit and Mosul under Maliki's guidance and under the leadership of the notorious General Qassem Soleimani. The elimination in Baghdad by the Americans of Soleimani and his ally the Iraqi Chief of Staff of Operations Abu Mehdi Mohandes, on 3rd January 2020, dealt a fatal blow to the Iranian regime. The US State Department listed Soleimani as an international terrorist. As the de-facto 2nd in command in Iran's military hierarchy after Supreme leader Khamenei, he was responsible for thousands of deaths among Iraqi, Syrian, and Lebanese people as well as among US military personnel. He controlled the Islamic Revolutionary Guards Corps (IRGC) Quds Force, their vicious unit responsible for extra-territorial operations. Soleimani was answerable only to Iran's Supreme Leader Ayatollah Khamenei and as such, was described by many as the second most powerful person in the Islamic Republic. As Quds Force commander, he oversaw the theocratic regime's proxy wars in Syria, Yemen, Lebanon and Iraq, where he commanded all the Iraqi militias. His death came as an irreparable blow to the clerical regime.

Khomeini created the IRGC as his own version of the Gestapo, to spread their revolutionary policy of violence and terror beyond Iran's borders. Soleimani played a pivotal role in this process. His poster still features on walls and hoardings across the Middle East. Following President Trumps withdrawal from the JCPOA nuclear deal and the re-imposition of tough sanctions, millions of Iranians took to the streets in 2018 protesting about the venal corruption of the ruling mullahs and their wanton spending on conflict and terror. In a blind panic, Khamenei instructed the IRGC to launch a murderous crackdown on the peaceful protesters, during which an estimated 1,500 were murdered, more than 4,000 were wounded and over 12,000 were arrested.

It should be noted that all the regime's factions, agencies, and forces are united in support of terrorism as a tool for projecting their malign power and this unity is institutionalized under the direction of the Supreme National Security Council (SNSC) that directs the overarching policy and execution. The SNSC in turn takes its orders directly from Khamenei and reports to him.

In times of national security crises, one important and often used tool has been to import and deploy Iraqi, Lebanese, and Afghan forces under the Quds Force command, to suppress Iranian protesters and to avoid complications with local forces. Soleimani played an instrumental role in this policy to deploy foreign mercenary forces. During the 2019 uprising as well, his forces received shoot-to-kill orders that saw masked snipers on the roofs of government buildings, indiscriminately shooting unarmed, young protesters in the head and chest. IRGC goons and security agents then scoured the country's hospitals, dragging the wounded from their beds.

The uprising was triggered by the regime's decision to triple the price of gasoline. This was the last straw for a nation whose citizens have been impoverished by the venally corrupt regime that for 40 years has stolen Iran's wealth for the benefit of its rulers and to finance proxy wars across the Middle East, where Soleimani oversaw Iranian support for Bashar al-Assad's bloody civil war in Syria, the brutal Houthi rebels in Yemen, the terrorist Hezbollah in Lebanon and the vicious Shi'a militias in Iraq.

Similar nationwide protests raged across Iraq in 2019, where young Iraqis demanded an end to Iranian interference in their country and the expulsion of Soleimani and his cohorts. In a chilling interview in 2019, Soleimani claimed "We know how to deal with protesters in Iran," as he deployed masked gunmen to murder hundreds of peaceful Iraqi demonstrators. It is no surprise that tens of thousands of young Iraqis took to the streets to celebrate Soleimani's and Abu Mehdi Mohandes' assassination.

Qassem Soleimani was one of the most vicious criminals in Iran's history. Pretending to aid the West in their war against ISIS, Soleimani oversaw the genocidal massacre of tens of thousands of Sunnis in the ancient Iraqi cities of Fallujah, Ramadi and Mosul, leaving smoking ruins in his wake. With his elimination, the process of overthrowing the mullahs and restoring peace, justice and democracy in Iran will be greatly expedited. The ayatollahs, with the direct involvement of their most powerful general, Qassem Soleimani, have committed appalling crimes against humanity that require an immediate response from the international community, involving, at the very least, a UN fact-finding mission to establish the truth about the numbers killed and injured in the 2019 nationwide uprising and to ascertain the treatment of those imprisoned. The UN must hold those responsible for these crimes accountable in the international courts of justice. As Qassem Soleimani and Abu Mehdi Mohandes discovered to their ultimate cost, there can be no impunity for those guilty of such chilling atrocities. The Americans eliminated a monster, and the world should be thankful.

Figure 24 - The terrorist Quds Force Commander – General Qassem Soleimani

Chapter Ten

GUNBOAT DIPLOMACY

Gunboat diplomacy is defined in terms of international politics as the pursuit of foreign policy objectives by displaying signs of aggressive naval power, implying the threat of warfare if agreeable terms are not met. Gunboat diplomacy was a tactic famously utilised by some of the imperialist powers during the nineteenth century. It is a somewhat outdated concept today, although that doesn't seem to have deterred the Iranian regime. In June 2022, ships from the US 5th Fleet were sailing through international waters in the Strait of Hormuz when they were threatened by high-speed, head-on assaults by three naval vessels from Iran's Islamic Revolutionary Guards Corps (IRGC). The US coastal patrol ship USS Sirocco had to fire a warning flare when the IRCC vessels, acting in a hostile manner, came within 50 yards of their ship. The threatening and dangerous behaviour lasted for more than one hour before the IRGC boats departed.

The Strait of Hormuz lies between the Persian Gulf and the Gulf of Oman, providing the only sea passage to the Indian Ocean for crude oil from many of the world's largest oil producers. An average of 21 million barrels a day flow through the strait, which is over 20 percent of global consumption. Around one third of the world's sea-borne petroleum and nearly all the liquefied gas from Qatar, the leading global gas exporter, passes through this constricted chokepoint only 21 miles wide at its narrowest point. With the ongoing global energy crisis caused by Russia's illegal invasion of Ukraine, the route has become even more strategically critical. As the theocratic regime faces crisis upon crisis at home and abroad, the elderly and fanatical Supreme Leader Ayatollah Ali Khamenei and his criminal president Ebrahim Raisi, have ramped up their aggressive activities in the Strait to frighten those they regard as the regime's enemies, even threatening to close the strait altogether.

The naval encounter in June 2022 was not the first. In June 2019, limpet mines were left behind by IRGC commandos following attacks on two oil tankers in the Gulf of Oman. The oil tanker Kokuka Courageous was rocked by several explosions which caused extensive damage. An IRGC patrol boat was then filmed moving alongside the tanker as commandos removed an unexploded limpet mine from the hull of the vessel. Following the attack, the Kokuka Courageous, along with the Norwegian-owned Front Altair, were towed to the Emirati coast by US naval authorities.

Figure 25 - The holed Kokuka Courageous in the Gulf of Oman

In July 2019, Iran seized the British-flagged Stena Impero on the Strait of Hormuz. It was held in the Iranian port of Bandar Abbas for two months and only released following international pressure. In January 2021, the IRGC seized a South Korean-flagged tanker in Gulf waters, claiming they had detained the Hankuk Chemi tanker and its crew for allegedly dumping toxic chemicals in the Gulf, a blatantly false accusation. In the same week, explosives experts had to defuse an Iranian limpet mine attached to a Liberian-flagged oil tanker in waters off the Iraqi port of Basra. Sailors on board the MT Pola said they had discovered a limpet mine of the type commonly deployed by naval divers. It had been attached to the side of the tanker and could have caused devastating damage had it exploded, particularly as the MT Pola was refuelling another tanker at the time with a ship-to-ship transfer to the MT Nordic Freedom, a Bermuda-flagged tanker.

In May 2021, an IRGC speedboat armed with heavy machine guns, approached within 150 yards of US warships at high speed, as the Americans travelled through the Strait of Hormuz. Warning shots had to be fired at the IRGC vessel before it finally withdrew. Then in August 2021 a tanker was hijacked by IRGC commandos and ordered to "sail to Iran" – days after an IRGC drone attack killed a British security guard working with special forces, and a Romanian soldier, on the MV Mercer Street. A nine-strong armed group climbed on board the Asphalt Princess off the coast of the Gulf of Oman, close to the Strait of Hormuz, seizing the vessel at gunpoint. The Iranian regime, as usual, denied involvement in the suspected drone attack and the hijacking.

The mullahs clearly believed that their aggressive conduct would lead to US capitulation over the stalled JCPOA nuclear talks. Using the IRGC to threaten shipping in the Strait of Hormuz was hardly likely to encourage American sympathy. Indeed, the US knows that the IRGC and its extra-territorial Quds Force is behind all the clerical regime's proxy wars in Syria, Yemen, Iraq, Lebanon, and Gaza and is known to sponsor international terror worldwide. The regime's foreign wars and acts of terror were an ongoing calculated strategy to distract their enraged and starving population from another nationwide uprising that could sweep the mullahs from power. The current nationwide insurrection has demonstrated clearly how this strategy has failed. Sham attempts at bullying the US into reinstating the nuclear deal were always doomed to fail, as were aggressive attempts to threaten international shipping in the Strait of Hormuz.

Chapter Eleven

IRAN'S MEDIEVAL PRISONS

The treatment of PMOI/MEK supporters who are arrested by the regime is brutal. Political prisoners in Tehran are systematically starved by the authorities to break their will and force them to repent. Terrified of every nationwide uprising that could sweep the theocratic dictatorship from power, the Ministry of Intelligence and Security (MOIS) ordered a severe crackdown on all inmates jailed for opposing the mullahs' regime. Thousands now suffer from severe food shortages in the medieval jails. Prisoners are given only 10 to 12 spoonfuls of low-quality rice daily. The rice is said to be stinking and rotten. Prisoners can purchase additional food at vastly inflated prices, but few can afford this luxury. Even the water supply in Tehran's prisons is contaminated, forcing prisoners to buy bottles of water at the punitive cost of 30,000 rials ($0.71c) per bottle. Many prisoners have no source of income whatsoever and having been the main breadwinners for their household, have left their families destitute and without income or food. The mental stress caused by their plight is used as a further source of torture by the venally corrupt prison officials. With more than 30,000 mostly young protesters detained during the current revolution, the prisons are bursting at the seams. But Iran's vast army of political prisoners can comfort themselves with the knowledge that the French Revolution began with the storming of the Bastille. Their day of freedom is imminent.

In the Greater Tehran Prison, solitary confinement as a punishment has been replaced with incarceration in large holding cells, designed for 20 prisoners, but now crammed with 60 to 70 people. There is a single toilet in the corner of each holding cell, obscured by a filthy curtain. The stench from the toilet constantly permeates the entire cell. There is no access to ventilation or direct sunlight and prisoners can be starved and held under these awful conditions for weeks, until their will is finally broken. Only then, after they have signed a commitment to repent their political views and have been forced to bow and grovel to the guards, are they returned to the public wards of the prison. There, at least they are allowed to go outside every morning into the sunlight from 7am to 8am, while a head count is undertaken.

Figure 26 - Evin Prison, Tehran

Much of the information on the brutal conditions in Tehran's medieval prisons has come from an audio file and letters smuggled out of the Greater Tehran Penitentiary by the fearless political prisoner Soheil Arabi, an Iranian blogger who was sentenced to death in 2013 for insulting the Prophet Mohammad in several Facebook postings. His sentence was commuted to a lengthy jail term and two years of mandatory study of Islamic theology. Arabi was awarded the Press Freedom Prize by Reporters Without Borders for his courageous attempts to draw attention on social media to the plight of Atena Daemi, the young female civil and children's rights activist, who has faced repeated torture and beatings and is serving a fourteen-year sentence for distributing anti-death penalty leaflets. Arabi has himself been subjected to repeated torture and beatings by the authorities for exposing the

Iranian regime's deplorable prison conditions. After he smuggled out his letters and audio tape denouncing the prison system to his family, his mother was arrested and charged with "disseminating propaganda against the state and in favour of dissident groups." Despite her frailty and poor health, she was severely tortured under interrogation and sentenced to 18-months imprisonment.

Soheil Arabi's bravery in exposing the inhumane prison conditions in Iran included a detailed description of the looting and rape that continues daily, with the full connivance of the prison guards. Arabi says that extortionist gangs and thieves, prey on newcomers in Tehran's jails, robbing them of any possession and often raping them. He says that this behaviour is not only tolerated, but openly encouraged by the prison guards and wardens. Monthly inspections are particularly cruel and sadistic. Military personnel from the IRGC assist prison officials in searching prisoners' cells and belongings, breaking dishes and flasks and responding to even the slightest complaint from a prisoner with violent beatings. Prisoners have been ordered not to look directly at the face of any soldiers during these inspections, presumably to avoid identification. Those who break this rule by raising their head are beaten unconscious with batons.

Conditions in Iran's women's prisons are equally dire. The infamous women's ward in Tehran's Evin Prison is divided into two halls, one for political prisoners and the other for the wives and children of male convicts. Clearly, none of these people should be in jail in the first place. Because of severe over-crowding, women sentenced for violent crimes or drug offences are being housed alongside political prisoners, leading to hostility and constant clashes.

Chapter Twelve

ASHRAF 3

The construction of this small city has become a source of inspiration for political dissidents in Iran. The hilly farmland purchased in September 2017 near the town of Manza, had no services and no infrastructure. It was barren agricultural land. Yet within months, the highly skilled and professional PMOI/MEK dissidents had installed water purification plants, electricity substations, sewerage works, roads and buildings to house 3,000 people. It was a miracle of construction and now this small city boasts massive meeting halls, a mosque, a museum, TV and Radio studios, a hospital and dental surgery, accommodation blocks and dormitories, shops, kitchens, bakeries, sports facilities, parks, flower beds, fountains, and statues. Ashraf 3 and its 3,000 residents are now the driving force behind the PMOI/MEK and a source of inspiration for millions of youngsters in Iran.

Figure 27 - Ashraf 3 – Albania – the birth of a new city

The tiny Balkans enclave of Albania, with a population of under three million, has once again shown the rest of the world what it means to offer a haven of safety and security to men, women and children fleeing from terror and repression. The Tirana government approved a request from the Biden administration to provide a home to Afghan interpreters and others who had helped US forces and who regarded America as their final destination. Edi Rama said that assisting people in need is a tradition in Albania and that he was happy to agree to Washington's request "Not just because our great allies ask us to, but because we are Albania." The 300 Afghan refugees who had arrived in Albania were housed in hotels on the Adriatic coast and on student campuses in the capital Tirana.

Albania's willingness to stick its head above the parapet came at a time of growing concern that NATO members weren't doing enough to offer protection to Afghans who feared reprisals from the Taliban. Iran, which initially agreed to welcome thousands of Afghan refugees, closed its borders, while Turkey constructed a three-metre-high wall along its border with Iran, to deter any Afghans who had managed to make the weeks-long journey through Iran to the Turkish border.

The EU decided to stop Afghan refugees from entering Europe en masse, amid fears of a repetition of the 2015 migration crisis, when over one million refugees came to the continent, mainly from the Middle East. An emergency meeting of EU home-affairs ministers in Brussels, as the Taliban takeover of Afghanistan unfolded, agreed to act jointly "to prevent the recurrence of uncontrolled, large-scale, illegal migration movements faced in the past." The Taliban announced, chillingly, that failed asylum seekers deported back to Afghanistan could face reprisals.

Albania's history of providing protection to those in need was amplified during the second world war. At that time the Albanian population numbered only around 800,000 of whom only 200 were Jews. But as the Nazis swept across Europe, Albania opened its doors to over 1,800 Jews from Germany, Austria, Serbia, Greece, and Yugoslavia, fleeing the holocaust. Following the German occupation of Albania in 1943, in an extraordinary demonstration of bravery, the Albanian population refused to hand over lists of Jews to the Nazis. This amazing act of resistance, by the only country in Europe that has a Muslim majority, was founded on the Albanian tradition of Besa, a code of honour that literally means "to keep the promise". It is a promise that the Albanians have kept to this day.

In March 2012, negotiations for the transfer of PMOI/MEK members from Iraq to Albania was launched by Lars Rise, a former member of the Norwegian parliament's foreign affairs committee and a friend of the organisation. Rise brought up the issue in a meeting with Albanian Prime Minister Sali Berisha who took a positive view of the matter. Representatives of the organization then raised the issue with the UNHCR and the US Government. In January 2013, Mohammad Mohaddessin and Mehdi Abrishamchi, representing the residents of Ashraf, and Lars Rise, met with the Albanian Prime Minister and committed to financially sponsor all the organisation's members to be transferred to Albania. The Albanian government agreed to an initial transfer of 210 of the Ashraf residents who were gradually transferred in 2013. In 2014 several hundred more were transferred.

The transfer process went very slowly while the Iranian regime's terrorist operations in Iraq against the MEK in Camp Liberty was continuously in progress. A savage missile attack on 28 October 2015 shocked the US, Albania, and the UN. Twenty-four residents of Camp Liberty were killed and vast swathes of the camp were destroyed. Subsequently, Prime Minister Edi Rama agreed to the transfer of the remaining 2,000 residents in 2016. The last group of residents left Camp Liberty near Baghdad and arrived in Albania on 9 September 2016.

Albania accepted some 3,000 members of the PMOI/MEK. Initially housed in apartment blocks in Tirana, the Iranian refugees were allowed to purchase farmland near the port of Durres, where they built an entire modern city, named Ashraf 3. The 3,000 Iranian dissidents, many of whom are highly educated intellectuals and academics, had lived as refugees in Iraq for almost three decades.

They were the targets of dozens of bloody attacks staged by Iranian sponsored terrorists in Iraq and even by Iraq's military on the orders of the Iraqi Prime Minister – Nouri al-Maliki, an Iranian puppet, with many of their number killed and wounded. Ashraf 3 in Albania rose from the ashes of Camps Ashraf and Liberty in Iraq. In Ashraf and Liberty, the PMOI/MEK women and men were attacked 29 times, resulting in 141 deaths, 1,400 wounded and 7 kidnapped, who have never been seen again. A further 27 Ashrafis died because of a medical blockade imposed by Nouri-al-Maliki and his leading henchman Faleh al-Fayadh.

Despite their plight and Iranian threats to annihilate them in Iraq, the EU and US were reluctant to offer them safe refuge. Once again, Albania stepped into the breach, agreeing to allow all 3,000 Iranians to settle in their country. The Albanian Interior Minister at that time - Samir Taheri – said in an interview: "We responded to a call for cooperation and humanity considering that the lives of these human beings were in danger. They are individuals facing serious threats in their home country. They are neither terrorists nor fundamentalists. They are people whose lives are in danger in their own land."

Against the background of violence and aggression that the Iranian dissidents had faced in Iraq, it was almost a miracle that tiny Albania was prepared to provide a safe haven for the PMOI/MEK refugees. The Albanians had suffered years of oppression under the communists, and they knew what it was like to fight for freedom and democracy. Their courage in rescuing the PMOI/MEK refugees from Iraq, caused a predictable backlash of fury from Tehran. The mullahs' regime began to beef up its embassy in Tirana, deploying dozens of diplomats with the key intention of targeting the PMOI/MEK. In December 2019, the Iranian ambassador to Albania and his first secretary, were expelled by Edi Rama and declared *personae non gratae* for "activities in breach of their diplomatic status and the Vienna Convention on Diplomatic Relations." They had been involved in a plot to attack the Iranian refugees in Ashraf 3. It was the second time a plot involving Iranian agents in Albania had been exposed. In March 2018, as mentioned in Chapter 9, Albanian police foiled a planned bomb attack on the exiled PMOI/MEK dissidents who were attending a Nowruz or New Year gathering in Tirana.

In September 2022, Albania severed all diplomatic ties with Iran and ordered the Iranian embassy staff to leave, accusing it of orchestrating a major cyber-attack. Prime Minister Edi Rama said a probe had found "incontrovertible evidence" that Iran "hired four groups to mount the attack on Albania" on 15 July. The hackers tried to paralyse public services, delete, and steal government data, and incite chaos, he added. Edi Rama's decisive action should be a clear lesson to Western nations on how to deal with the theocratic regime and its so-called diplomatic staff.

Chapter Thirteen

THE TATTERED NUCLEAR DEAL

Signed with the Iranian regime in 2015 by America, Russia, China, France, Germany and Britain, the so-called Joint Comprehensive Plan of Action (JCPOA), masterminded by Barack Obama as his last-ditch keynote foreign policy achievement, was a failure from the outset. Obama naively believed that the release of $150 billion of frozen Iranian assets, as part of the nuclear agreement, would put bread back on the table for Iran's starving citizens. Instead, the mullahs diverted most of the cash to funding Bashar al-Assad's brutal civil war in Syria, with additional resources split between the Houthi rebels in Yemen, the terrorist Hezbollah in Lebanon, Hamas in Palestine and the vicious Shi'a militias in Iraq. The little money that was left was funnelled, as usual, into the ayatollahs' personal bank accounts. The Iranian people got nothing.

Figure 28 - The Joint Commission overseeing the JCPOA nuclear deal in Vienna

Obama also conceded that Iran's expanding ballistic missile program should be left out of the nuclear deal, even though the regime was known to have missiles capable of carrying nuclear warheads and striking targets in Israel, Saudi Arabia or even Europe. North Korea has been an active partner with the Iranian regime in supplying weapons technology. Vladimir Putin has also delivered S-300 surface to air missile systems to Iran. History has repeatedly demonstrated that countries that wish to undertake the vast expense and risk the international criticism of developing intercontinental ballistic missiles do so because they intend to arm their missiles with nuclear warheads and become nuclear powers. The Iranian missile program makes no military, political or economic sense unless viewed in this context.

President Obama's former top military intelligence official – Retired Lt. Gen. Michael Flynn – former head of the Defense Intelligence Agency, told the House Foreign Affairs subcommittee in Washington in early June 2015 that any nuclear deal with Iran could only be a "placeholder" based on "wishful thinking". He said the only way to stop Iran's nuclear program was "regime change". Flynn said that any nuclear deal with Iran would set off a domino effect across the Middle East, with countries like Saudi Arabia rushing to buy nuclear weapons technology from Pakistan or other nuclear nations. The Saudi Ambassador to the UK also stated that "all the options are on the table," including the possibility that the kingdom could take possession of nuclear weapons from Pakistan. These weapons were readily accessible to the Saudis due to their cooperation and support for Pakistan's military program.

So, the nuclear deal was deeply flawed. It forbade inspectors from the International Atomic Energy Agency (IAEA) from inspecting any sites controlled by the military inside Iran. Virtually all the theocratic regime's secret nuclear programme was being developed in military sites run by the IRGC, so the deal was defective from the outset. Page after page of the JCPOA read like a telephone directory, listing names of Iranian companies and individuals from whom all sanctions were to be lifted, including business and industries like banking, insurance, metals, aviation, shipping, arms, and general trade markets, even covering the re-opening of Iran's right to sell carpets and caviar to the West. Ludicrously, Obama's deal even ordered the West to end its "exclusion of Iranian citizens from higher education coursework related to careers in nuclear science, nuclear engineering or the energy sector." In other words, Western universities would be encouraged to train Iranians in advanced nuclear technology to ensure that they were properly equipped to build a nuclear bomb! Donald Trump denounced the deal even before he became president and withdrew America from the JCPOA unilaterally in May 2018.

Figure 29 - Mike Pompeo – US Secretary of State under President Donald Trump

Trumps' withdrawal from the deal coincided with a re-imposition of tough sanctions in what he termed his 'maximum pressure' campaign. Trump's secretary of state, Mike Pompeo, emphasized that any return to the JCPOA would involve mandatory inspections at all sites requested by international inspectors, while ensuring that Iran never came close to possessing a nuclear weapon. Unlike the flawed Obama nuclear deal, Pompeo insisted that the provisions in the JCPOA must have no expiration date and Iran's development and testing of ballistic missiles must be subject to severe sanctions. Pompeo also demanded an end to the theocratic regime's financing and support for proxy wars across the Middle East, an end to its sponsorship of international terror and for major improvements to its human rights record in Iran.

The EU and its then top diplomat Federica Mogherini, went into meltdown at the US withdrawal from the JCPOA, repeatedly assuring the mullahs that they supported the deal and were doing everything possible to navigate their way around Trump's US sanctions. Mogherini visited Tehran, wore the headscarf in simpering acquiescence to the mullahs' misogyny and even posed for selfies with turbaned members of the Iranian parliament. When Mogherini was replaced by Josep Borrell, the socialist former foreign minister of Spain, things got even worse. Borrell even sent his deputy, Enrique Mora, to Tehran to attend the inauguration as president on 5th August 2021 of Ebrahim Raisi, the so-called 'Butcher of Tehran'. The inauguration ceremony took place less than a week after a British and a Romanian national were killed in an Iranian drone strike on an Israel-operated oil tanker in the Arabian sea, about which Borrell made no comment.

Israel slammed the decision of the European Union to send a senior diplomat to the swearing-in ceremony calling it "shameful, puzzling, and showing poor judgment." Israeli Foreign Ministry spokesperson Lior Haiat said: "The participation of the EU representative in the ceremony comes just a few days after Iran killed two civilians, one of whom was from an EU member State, in an act of state terrorism against civilian shipping."

Talks in Vienna have stalled at Iran's insistence that all sanctions imposed by former president Donald Trump under his 'maximum pressure' campaign must be lifted, including those that were directed at the regime's proxy wars in the Middle East, which is something Biden, politically, cannot entertain. They also want a guarantee that no future US administration would ever again withdraw from the deal, a guarantee that no president is able to give. Khamenei also insists the US must remove the IRGC from its Foreign Terrorist list. Meanwhile the mullahs have accelerated their program of enriching uranium, now at 90% purity, which is only a technical step away from weapons grade. They have torn down surveillance cameras installed by the International Atomic Energy Agency (IAEA). Their clear objective is to build a nuclear bomb and their pretext of negotiations in Vienna were only ever a masquerade to hide that reality from the West.

Russia, as a signatory to the original 2015 JCPOA, must give its consent to any renewal. There can be no credibility in any treaty signed by Putin. He has proved himself to be a liar, a cheat, a swindler, a gangster and now a mass murderer, who happily ignores the UN Charter and even tramples over the Geneva Convention for humanitarian standards in war. Putin's ruthless targeting of the civilian population in Ukraine has turned him into another Hitler. There can surely be no question of signing any agreement with such a monster. But now Russia has added its own list of demands to the revised JCPOA. Maria Zakharova, a spokesperson for the Russian Foreign Ministry, said on 16th March 2022 that Moscow wanted additional provisions in the deal covering future cooperation between Moscow and Tehran on nuclear projects. She blamed "hostile attacks of the United States and the European Union on Russia" for the request.

For almost 80 years the West has allowed itself to slumber. We celebrated the collapse of the Soviet Union and the end of the Cold War with decades of reduced military spending, convinced that the world had become a more tolerant and democratic place. The invasion of Ukraine and the horrifying spectacle of war and suffering in Europe has jolted our generation out of its torpor. We now recognise that while we slept, Putin was planning his genocidal aggression. The forces of good must once again align against the forces of evil. The West must tear up the Iranian nuclear deal and slam the door on Putin and his allies. Murderous dictators like Ebrahim Raisi, the president of Iran and Vladimir Putin, the president of Russia, should be indicted for crimes against humanity and genocide and tried in the International Criminal Court in the Hague.

Despite Tehran's official statements about aiming to resume the nuclear talks with the P4+1, as well as negotiating indirectly about sanction relief with Washington, following the election of President Biden, Ebrahim Raisi's nuclear team did nothing but waste time in eight lengthy rounds in Vienna and Doha and practically killed hopes of any JCPOA revival. The regime overplayed its hand in the negotiations and thought it could force a war-fatigued Washington to concede everything on its wish list. Though the truth about Tehran's ailing status at home and abroad was too visible for the West to surrender one-sidedly and the regime intensified its extortion tactics through nuclear advancements and reducing cooperation with the UN's nuclear watchdog.

The IAEA Board of Governors censured the Iranian regime on June 8, 2022. Solely relying on Russia and China's veto power in the United Nations Security Council, the regime tried desperately to incentivize both regimes to shield itself against a potential UNSC Resolution Charter 7. Wary of more exposure or military attacks against its nuclear sites, the regime began openly threatening to build nuclear warheads. Multiple state officials constantly expressed warnings, keen to convey the message that Tehran has already joined the nuclear club and the world has no other option but to surrender to the regime's blackmail. At the time of writing the JCPOA remains moribund. A leading article in The Times on 17th January 2023 – entitled 'Barbaric Regime' set out the definitive position on the JCPOA. The article stated: "Tehran cheated while the deal was in force in order to approach nuclear weapons capability. Now it is easy for Tehran to string the West along, building up its nuclear capability, while seeking to persuade the West it has done enough to justify sanctions relief." The article concluded: "Besides, the spreading domestic revolt in Iran, and its brutal suppression, have made it impossible to treat the regime as a potential partner. Britain should abandon a fruitless policy of "pretend and extend", that is, pretending Iran is acting in good faith on nuclear weapons, while extending the offer to lift western sanctions. Instead, it should speak clearly, preferably within days. The Revolutionary Guards should be declared a terrorist organisation and banned from Britain. It is the biggest arms supplier of Hezbollah, which is already banned here. It promotes hostile, extremist propaganda. It has no place in this country."

Chapter Fourteen

POVERTY AND UNREST

Sixty million Iranians, 75% of the population, are now living below the international poverty line. The grinding privation and penury has driven people to sell their kidneys and even their corneas for cash. Evil organ traders are exploiting the poor to rake in huge profits. The Iranian currency - the rial – is in freefall. It lost 49% of its value in just 12 months. Iran, as one of the world's leading oil and gas producers, now has one of the world's most worthless currencies, with hyper-inflation topping 52.2% annually. Four decades of venal corruption, dim-witted incompetence and brutal oppression by the fascist Iranian government has brought this once prosperous and successful nation to its knees.

Figure 30 - Poverty and despair in Iran

The despair and anger of the population has been compounded by the regime's incompetent handling of the coronavirus pandemic. A new wave of covid swept across Iran in the summer of 2022, adding to the woes of the troubled Islamic state. Although the theocratic regime claimed the death toll was 142,000, it is believed that more than 530,000 people have died in Iran so far due to the pandemic.[82] The lack of viable vaccines and shortage of medical equipment opened the floodgates to a resurgence of infection. The Supreme Leader Ayatollah Ali Khamenei's opposition to western vaccines, relying instead on Russian and Chinese alternatives, left the Iranian population defenceless in the face of new coronavirus variants which spread rapidly.

According to the regime's Health Ministry in July 2022, the daily death toll from Covid-19 led to four cities being registered as highly infective red zones, while 14 were designated as orange and 142 as yellow. The dean of the Mashhad Medical Apparatus Organization said: "In the worst-case scenario, we will witness a new coronavirus peak near mid-August. A more realistic estimate tells us the peak will be seen in September and October." The state-run Khabar Online website reported: "We are returning to the dreadful days of living with Covid-19. The intense days when not one single empty bed or a few meters of space was found for a patient, when finding an oxygen device relied on a miracle."

The true extent of the death toll in Iran was gathered by resistance units of the PMOI/MEK. They reiterated that the mullahs' venal corruption and incompetence had caused a catastrophic covid meltdown across the country, with the highly contagious BA.4 and BA.5 strands of the virus spreading like wildfire against the largely un-vaccinated population. Iran's hospitals had few resources available to provide treatment. Hospital staff were left without personal protective equipment (PPE), which had been sold on the black market by officials from the IRGC.

---

[82] See, for example, "Iran's COVID-19 deaths '2.5 times higher' than health ministry numbers," Atlantic Council, December 1, 2021.

Iran's monetary and financial institutions are in the hands of the regime's corrupt leaders. On 28 February 1979, immediately following the revolution, the regime established the Foundation of the Underprivileged. 28 private banks and industries covering steel, aluminium and vehicles were all confiscated by the State, together with the properties of all the biggest businessmen, who were the backbone of the Iranian economy. All were nationalized and handed over to the Foundation of the Underprivileged, which was wholly controlled by the Supreme Leader Ayatollah Khomeini. In 2013, this foundation was valued at $95 bn. All foundations like this get their funding directly from the government. They don't pay tax and they have no accountability on how they spend their money. The IRGC also has a tight grip on these foundations. Iran has used the construction companies under the control of these foundations to spread the Islamic revolution in countries across the Middle East. These IRGC construction companies also run missile factories.

The IRGC's stranglehold on the Iranian economy has been disastrous. There are currently around 75,000 unfinished construction projects in Iran. Money is allocated annually, but never spent on these projects. The regime owes 25 trillion rials to contractors ($150 bn). So, the government has been held hostage by the IRGC for years because of these escalating debts. The resulting devastation of Iran's production capabilities has been massive. 38 cotton companies closed in 2018. 1,000 factory units building fridges, TVs and producing textiles have also closed down. Mass unemployment has been the inevitable result. There are 1.2 million more unemployed people in Iran every year, mostly young people. The regime's own statistics say the average monthly wage of a worker today is only enough to last for one week. 20,000 people are sleeping rough in Tehran alone, of which 5,000 are women.

The IMF said that in 2018 Iran had 1.5% negative growth. They predicted 3.6% negative growth in 2019 and a decrease of $97 bn in GDP. The regimes system of velayat-e-faqih, the guardianship of the Islamic jurist, offers no solution to the economic crisis. The whole Iranian economy is focused on the military requirements of the IRGC. Iranian society is facing chaos. The capacity of the regime to reform the economy is no longer there. Instead, the mullahs turn their attention to demonizing the main democratic opposition movement, the PMOI, to hide the reality of their economic mismanagement. That is why the protesters on the streets of every town and city in Iran can be heard shouting "Death to this deceiving government."

The seething resentment and antipathy to the clerical regime has begun to boil over. Poverty-stricken Iranians are appalled that their government continues to pour money and military personnel into Syria in support of Bashar al-Assad's bloody civil war. They are horrified that the mullahs are funnelling endless Iranian cash to the Houthi rebels in Yemen, Hezbollah in Lebanon and the vicious Shi'a militias in Iraq. They are shocked to learn that vast resources are being channelled into the secret production of nuclear weapons and ballistic missiles, despite international denials.

Figure 31 - Mass protests in Iran

The unrest exploded into a nationwide insurrection in September 2022 following the murder of the young Kurdish girl Mahsa Amini by the so-called 'morality police,' for not wearing her hijab properly.

PMOI/MEK Resistance Units have burgeoned in towns and cities across Iran. Young PMOI/MEK Resistance fighters have attacked IRGC and Basij bases throughout Iran. A centre for promoting fundamentalist Islam was torched in the city of Karaj. Banners, posters and images of Iran's Supreme Leader, and of the terrorist IRGC Quds Force General Qassem Soleimani, killed by a drone strike in January 2020, have been repeatedly targeted and set on fire by protesters. Marchers in street protests routinely chant slogans such as "The Supreme Leader's end is near." Anti-regime slogans and messages from the Iranian Resistance leader Massoud Rajavi, and President-elect of the NCRI, Maryam Rajavi, regularly appear on walls and hoardings. In Karaj, brave young resistance fighters set fire to the Basij 'Women's Unit' headquarters. The "women's unit" is particularly detested for its role in enforcing the theocratic regime's misogynistic dress and behaviour laws. They are notorious for vicious crackdowns on women and girls who stand up for their rights and defy the strict hijab rules.

As resistance to the mullahs has spread across Iran, there are increasing demands for the international community to end their policy of appeasement and show their support for the Iranian people. The on-going torture and execution of political prisoners is a crime against humanity and continues because, to this date, the UN has singularly failed to hold the mullahs' regime to account for the massacre of over 30,000 political prisoners, mostly supporters of the PMOI/MEK, in 1988.

The unfolding revolution is the inevitable culmination of years of mounting protests against the theocratic regime. The killing by the IRGC of fuel porters in Sistan and Baluchestan province in February 2021, triggered widespread unrest that went on for weeks, despite a brutal crackdown by the authorities and a province-wide internet blackout. In July 2021, the clerical regime ordered the IRGC to open fire on unarmed civilian demonstrators in Khuzestan province who were protesting at on-going power cuts during the intense summer heatwave. Dozens were killed. By November, tens of thousands of farmers in Isfahan had joined a mass protest over the desiccation of the Zayandeh Rud river, depriving them of essential irrigation resources for their crops. The farmers blamed the IRGC for diverting water from the river to neighbouring Yazd province, where they have corruptly plundered the profits from a series of heavy industrial, water-guzzling, military factories. Once again, the protesters were violently attacked with batons and tear gas. The IRGC also opened fire with shotguns, wounding over 300 farmers, many of whom were struck in the face with shotgun pellets and lost one or both eyes. Protesters across the whole of Iran began wearing eye-patches over one eye in sympathy with their wounded compatriots.

Figure 32 - The desiccation of the Zayandeh Rud River

As the year 2021 ended, tens of thousands of teachers took to the streets in towns and cities across Iran, protesting about legislation that only allocated a fraction of the budget required to meet their needs and left most of them in extreme poverty. The nationwide protests were joined by impoverished workers and pensioners, defrauded investors, frustrated students, angry health workers and ordinary citizens dismayed at the spiralling inflation and collapsing economy. Deaths from the coronavirus pandemic reached an appalling 500,000. There was a growing realization that the venal corruption and rank incompetence of the ruling mullahs had taken Iran to breaking point. 80 million beleaguered Iranians knew that their once wealthy country has been plundered by the mullahs to finance their proxy wars in the Middle East. They knew that while they starved, billions of dollars were beings squandered on the bid to build a nuclear bomb and the ballistic missile systems required to carry it. Despite the economic meltdown, Ebrahim Raisi presented a budget from 2023 that posited a massive increase in funding for the IRGC and Basij, allocating at least $5 billion to boost the regime's so-called "defense capacities and strategic research," up from $4 billion the previous year.

The new year dawned with the unfolding revolution in Iran entering its most critical stage. The nationwide insurrection has continued for months showing no sign of subsiding, despite a ruthless crackdown by the theocratic regime's security forces, which has seen more than 750 protesters killed and over 30,000 arrested. Strikes and protests have crippled the Iranian economy, already reeling from years of tough Western sanctions. Now the Iranian currency has nose-dived to its lowest level ever against the US dollar. When the uprising began in September, following the death in custody of Mahsa Amini, the rial was trading at 315,000 to the dollar. In January 2023 it plummeted to 430,000 to the dollar. In desperation, the mullahs sacked Ali Salehabadi, head of the central bank and replaced him with Mohammad Reza Farzin, the 57-year-old senior banker and former deputy finance minister. Farzin has inherited a poisoned chalice. He can do nothing to prevent the rial from collapsing.

Iran now faces hyperinflation, similar to what occurred in the Weimar Republic of Germany between 1921-1923, when accelerating inflation rapidly eroded the value of the local currency, forcing the price of everything to rocket. The Weimar government began printing more and more paper Marks until barrow-loads were required to purchase a single loaf of bread. The government was then unable to meet its operating costs by raising taxes, because these taxes would have to be paid in the ever-falling German currency. The political leaders were faced with two unacceptable alternatives. Either they could stop inflation, causing immediate bankruptcies, unemployment, strikes, hunger, violence, the collapse of civil order, insurrection and revolution, or if they allowed inflation to continue, they would inevitably default on their foreign debt. Ultimately, they suffered both and the Weimar Republic collapsed. A similar fate now beckons for the mullahs' tyrannical dictatorship. They cannot survive.

The mullahs are now attempting to shore up their disintegrating economy by selling scores of small kamikaze 'Shahed' killer drones to Vladimir Putin, for use in his genocidal war in Ukraine. The drones are not much larger than ones that can be purchased for children in the West and are relatively cheap to build at around $6,000 each. They are, however, lethally effective and can find and destroy a target many miles away in minutes. Putin has replaced his dwindling stockpile of missiles with the Iranian regime's kamikaze drones, targeting Ukraine's electricity and gas generators and power stations, in an attempt to freeze the Ukrainian population into submission during the harshest months of winter. In his January 2023 visit to Washington DC, Volodymyr Zelensky, the Ukrainian president, condemned the mullahs for supporting Russia in the Ukrainian conflict. During a speech to Congress, Zelensky said Iranian drones sent to Russia had become a "threat to our critical infrastructure." He continued: "When Russia cannot reach our cities by its artillery, it tries to destroy them with missile attacks. More than that, Russia found an ally in this genocidal policy - Iran. That is how one terrorist has found the other."

The Iranian regime, past masters at lying and dissembling, quickly tried to deny Zelensky's allegations. Naser Kanani, a spokesman for the mullahs' foreign ministry described the Ukrainian president's claim as a "baseless accusation", stating: "We have always respected the territorial integrity of other countries, including Ukraine, and Mr Zelenskyy should know that Iran's strategic patience for baseless accusations will not be unlimited. We emphasize once again that the Islamic Republic of Iran has not exported any military equipment to any side for use in the Ukraine war."

Meanwhile, in response to international demands for severe action against the Islamic Revolutionary Guards Corps (IRGC) – the regime's Gestapo, the British government has declared that it will consider blacklisting the organisation as a terrorist group, meaning that it will become a criminal offence to belong to the IRGC, attend its meetings or even carry its logo. It is the IRGC's brutal response to the nationwide uprising that has given rise to the UN Security Council, Amnesty International, Human Rights Watch and others, calling for retaliatory action from the West. The IRGC's shoot to kill strategy has led to the death of hundreds of innocent men, women and even minors, during the ongoing disturbances. The blacklisting by the UK government is supported by Britain's security minister, Tom Tugendhat, and Home Secretary Suella Braverman and will come as a deadly blow to the Iranian regime, who rely on the IRGC for overseas trade.

One by one the dominoes are falling and like the Weimar Republic, the mullahs will no longer be able to cling to power. Whereas the Weimar Republic was Germany's first experiment with democracy and its collapse led to an era of fascism and World War II, the exact opposite is happening in the Islamic Republic of Iran, where an era of fascist, theocratic tyranny and repression is about to be overthrown and replaced by a democratically elected government. Eighty million Iranians have had enough. After four decades of tyranny and repression they are chanting "death to the dictator and death to Khamenei", the regime's elderly and delusional Supreme Leader, on the streets. What began as a demand for freedom has rapidly evolved into a revolutionary ultimatum for regime change. The mostly young protesters, led and coordinated by Resistance Units of the PMOI/MEK, the main democratic opposition movement, have lost their fear of the regime's brutal security forces. Gunfire, teargas, baton charges, arrest, torture, imprisonment and execution have simply fired their passion and inspired escalating reprisals against the mullahs' regime. 100 years after the collapse of the Weimar Republic, history is repeating itself and for Iranians, a better future will be the prize. Raisi's insulting budget, massively increasing funds for the IRGC and Basij, while failing to meet the needs of Iran's poverty-stricken population, is the last nail in the tyrannical regime's coffin.

Instead of confronting these challenges and seeking to resolve them, the knee-jerk reaction of the elderly Supreme Leader Ayatollah Ali Khamenei has been to order more repression, more arrests, more executions and an increased utilization of intimidation and assassination of dissidents and critics abroad. The execution of the dual British/Iranian citizen Alireza Akbari in January 2023 was an act of appalling barbarity that attracted international condemnation and effectively ended further hopes of resurrecting the mothballed nuclear talks.

The theocratic regime is in a dangerously unstable state. The Supreme Leader, Ali Khamenei and his army of venally corrupt and sociopathic mullahs, are terrified that the current nationwide uprising could throw them from power. The mullahs and their IRGC flunkies have wrecked the Iranian economy. With inflation running at around 50.5 percent, 80 million Iranians are now facing abject poverty and destitution. 70% of the Iranian population now live below the extreme international poverty line of $1 per day. They face starvation and a daily struggle to survive.

As acute poverty deepens, the corruption of the mullahs and their IRGC protectors, becomes increasingly apparent. Senior mullahs, members of the judiciary and IRGC commanders now live in excessive luxury. A powerful system of political patronage, nepotism, cronyism, plundering and embezzlement, sustains the elite and cripples the economy, effectively stealing bread from the mouths of the people.

The mullahs seized on concerns about a fifth wave of the coronavirus as a convenient excuse to explain the disastrous turnout at the sham presidential elections on 18th June 2021. Khamenei had engineered his favoured candidate, Ebrahim Raisi, into pole position to win the presidency, having disqualified all the other likely contenders. But the Iranian public despised Raisi, the head of the Judiciary, as a thug and mass murderer and were aware of his background as a key executioner during the horrific 1988 massacre of 30,000 political prisoners. That's why they boycotted the election in unprecedented numbers.

Chapter Fifteen

THE PLIGHT OF WOMEN IN IRAN

There are approximately 40 million women in the Islamic Republic of Iran, over half under the age of thirty. At a time when women in the West have achieved political, economic, personal and social equality, Iranian women are amongst the most repressed in the world, ruled by a regime dominated by elderly, bearded misogynists. It is little wonder that the current nationwide protests, which have continued in almost every town and city in Iran for many months, have often been led by or involved the participation of thousands of women, chanting "With hijab or without hijab, we march to revolution". Female teachers, medical staff, students, factory workers and pensioners have taken to the streets to demand an end to corruption, an end to discrimination and repression and an end to the clerical regime's aggressive military adventurism across the middle East. The chants of the protesters openly call for regime change. Many of these courageous women have been inspired by the PMOI/MEK and its charismatic leader Mrs Maryam Rajavi. Indeed, many of the key leadership positions within the PMOI/MEK are held by powerful and resilient women.

The theocratic dictatorship in Iran has a history of targeting women with oppressive laws that would not be tolerated in the West or indeed in most countries in the world. In Iran women are considered the property of their closest male relative and have no legal rights. Girls of nine can be married off by their parents. A woman's evidence in court is worth only half that of a man. Women may not seek to have a man charged with rape unless they have four independent witnesses. All family relationships are strictly controlled by Shariah law. Homosexual behaviour, adultery, sex outside marriage, are all prohibited. Women accused of such behaviour can incur severe punishments, including beatings and death, sometimes by stoning.

Seventeen years before the 1979 Islamic revolution, Ayatollah Khomeini wrote to the Shah saying that the "interests of the state are better served by preserving the religious teachings of Islam and calmness of the heart". He concluded the letter by advising the Shah that the right for women to vote should not be allowed. Khomeini stated that equality between women and men was "in fundamental violation of some of the most crucial rulings of Islam and in defiance of some of the explicit commandments of the Quran". Immediately following the revolution, Khomeini abolished the 'Family Protection Law' that gave women family rights. He also cancelled social services for women and abolished the role of female judges in Iran's justice system. It is perhaps not surprising that the Majlis passed a law banning women from riding bicycles!

Women's dress codes are also under constant scrutiny. They must wear the hijab and 'morality police' are on constant patrol to enforce the law. Women, particularly young women, are singled out for brutal attacks for the 'crime' of mal veiling, as in the case of the brutal killing of Mahsa Amini by the morality police in September 2022.

In 1988 the mullahs massacred over 30,000 political prisoners, most of whom were supporters of the PMOI/MEK. Tens of thousands of those hanged, day after day, were grandmothers, mothers, pregnant women and even teenagers. Senior members of the Iranian government have boasted of their role in this appalling crime against humanity, which has been the subject of reports by Amnesty international and is actively being investigated by the UN. Now the fascist mullah regime has turned its wrath on female human rights activists and even environmentalists, who are routinely rounded up by the regime's Gestapo, the IRGC, tortured and imprisoned.

In a pledge to Mrs Maryam Rajavi, leader of the PMOI/MEK in April 2018, Anissa Boumediene, the former first lady of Algeria, said: "Yes, we stand with you Maryam, as we stand with all our Iranian sisters, in your fierce fight seeking to free Iranian women from what enchains and imprisons them." Her words should resonate in the West, where female politicians and activists must show solidarity with their oppressed and brutalised Iranian sisters, by backing the main democratic opposition movement and fighting for freedom, justice, human rights and women's rights and a better future for Iran's daughters, grand-daughters and all Iranians. Indeed, it was incredibly brave of the European Parliament's president – Roberta Metsola – to address a huge crowd of anti-Iranian regime protesters in Strasbourg in January 2023, telling them that as the representative of 500 million Europeans, she pledged her support for the brave women and men taking to the streets in Iran, chanting 'Women-Life-Freedom.'

Figure 33 - Roberta Metsola – President of the European Parliament.

Chapter Sixteen

THE PLIGHT OF CHILDREN IN IRAN

The plight of children in Iran has become an international scandal. Nelson Mandela said "The true character of a society is revealed in how it treats its children." The true character of the fascist dictatorship that rules Iran was certainly revealed during the coronavirus pandemic. While scientists across the world agreed that children appeared to be less vulnerable to Covid-19 than adults, in Iran, the mullahs shamefully blamed street children for spreading the disease, exposing these vulnerable children to further hatred and abuse.

There are an estimated 33,000 destitute street children, sleeping rough in Iran's towns and cities. They range in age from 5 to 18. They are starved and abused and forced to sleep on the same streets where they try to eke out a paltry living selling flowers, gum, washing car windows and grabbing any chance of menial labour to survive. The Islamic Republic of Iran signed the UN Convention on the Rights of the Child (CRC) in 1991, and ratified it in 1994. Typically, upon ratification, the clerical regime made the following reservation: "If the text of the Convention is or becomes incompatible with the domestic laws and Islamic standards at any time or in any case, the Government of the Islamic Republic shall not abide by it." With this religious loophole as a blatant get-out clause, the Islamic Republic of Iran has repeatedly violated its obligations under the treaty and has been routinely criticized by foreign governments and international human rights organisations.

A notorious video recorded in Tehran in 2018 by a member of the brutal Basij internal security forces, showed two terrified children, no more than 6 or 7 years old, being forced to eat the flowers they were trying to sell on the streets, including their plastic coverings. The Basij thug had apprehended the kids for illegal street trading and proudly recorded the video to post on social media, as a warning to other children against breaking the law. In the deeply disturbing film, the Basij thug can be heard shouting threateningly "Eat it, eat it" at the petrified children, as they struggle to chew and swallow the plastic-wrapped flowers, choking and gagging in distress. This is how the Iranian regime treats its deprived kids. The governments of most civilized nations would deem feeding any starving children as a priority. But the repressive mullahs' regime regards them with derision as some sort of contaminant to be cleansed from the streets.

Figure 34 - Children in poverty in Iran

Some brave human rights activists inside Iran estimate that there are now millions of child laborers in the country. Deprived of even basic welfare, they are forced to work for a pittance to avoid death from starvation. Many children can be seen rummaging through garbage bins and landfill dumps, looking for items to eat or to sell.

Iran's children are the unwitting victims of this chaos, forced to take to the streets in search of money for a day's meagre meal, they are routinely exploited by child traffickers. Many are forced into drug use, and more are sexually abused and raped, subsequently falling into life-long drug addiction. Any country's future relies on its children and the mullahs are destroying that future. There is no fear that any of Nelson Mandela's wisdom and vision will ever have penetrated the medieval minds of the mullahs. The only hope for the future is the rapid removal of this malevolent regime, with the active assistance of the PMOI/MEK.

Courageous resistance units of the PMOI/MEK have helped to fan the flames of the ongoing protest and insurrection in towns and cities across Iran, daubing graffiti on walls and defacing government buildings and effigies of Khamenei and Ebrahim Raisi, the Iranian president, dubbed 'the butcher of Tehran'. State-controlled TV and Radio broadcasts have been repeatedly interrupted by resistance unit cyber operations, displaying images of Mrs Maryam Rajavi, and calling for the downfall of Khamenei, Raisi and their henchmen.

80 million beleaguered Iranians know that their once wealthy country has been plundered by the mullahs and their rage has reached boiling point. No amount of repression, brutality, arrests, imprisonment, torture, and executions can quell the rising tide of opposition to one of the world's most evil regimes. With more than half of its cooking oil imported from Ukraine and half of its wheat coming from Russia, Putin's illegal invasion and ongoing war has brought supplies almost to a standstill. IRGC gangsters are selling Iran's heavily subsidized stocks of bread to neighbouring Iraq and Afghanistan and pocketing the proceeds, spiking widespread hunger and fury in Iran. Drought and Western sanctions have further ravaged the Iranian economy which is now teetering on the edge of collapse. Desperate to sell condensate to Venezuela, the mullahs have even despatched Iranian-flagged vessels to trans-ship cargoes of the light oil onto sanction-busting Venezuelan tankers in remote parts of the Indian Ocean near the Maldives, from where they head home to the Bolivarian Republic in Latin America. The cash-strapped Venezuelans require loads of Iranian condensate to convert their extra heavy oil, to boost exports.

Chapter Seventeen

DESTROYING THE ENVIRONMENT

Prior to the 1979 revolution, Iran's population, numbering 34 million people at that time, relied on a stable water supply, sourced from millennia-old underground canals and aquifers. The Islamic revolution, highjacked by the mullahs, changed all that. The theocratic regime handed control of the nationalized water industry and indeed over 50% of all other business, industrial and service sectors, to the IRGC and Iran now faces an ecological disaster. The mullahs' maladministration over four decades has left Iran struggling with deforestation, desertification, water scarcity and countless other examples of environmental degradation. Climate change is exacerbating these environmental issues and turning them into a matter of life and death for the Iranian population. The deprived people living in southern, central and eastern Iran have witnessed the relentless destruction of their water infrastructure by the regime's institutions, primarily the IRGC. The situation has become so bad that in Sistan and Baluchistan province in south-eastern Iran, people are being forced to collect rainwater from ditches and from crocodile infested lakes. In Lorestan in 2020, the CEO of the Water & Sewerage Company claimed that only half of the villages in his district are even linked to water and sewer systems. The MP for Ahwaz, in southwest Iran, claimed that 800 villages in his area had no access to drinking water, even although there were five large dams and seven rivers nearby.

Many dams have been constructed by the IRGC in the wrong places, preventing water from reaching towns and villages and causing drought in some areas and flooding in others. Farmers, deprived of a regular water supply are no longer able to irrigate their crops, creating food shortages. Meanwhile corrupt IRGC officials pocket the profits from selling potable water at outrageous prices to some of Iran's poorest people. As always, when sporadic protests break out, the regime refuses to help, instead ordering the IRGC and Basij internal security thugs to crackdown on protesters and crush dissent, turning Iran into a volatile powder-keg, that has now exploded into open insurrection.

Combining rank incompetence, venal corruption, and a total disregard for environmental concerns, the IRGC set about a decades' long program of widespread hydropower dam building, in a series of huge and dishonestly lucrative infrastructure projects, that blocked and diverted rivers and drained lakes and aquifers. As the population of Iran expanded exponentially to its current 83 million and climate change saw summer temperatures often soaring to 50 degrees Celsius (122°F), the water crisis grew. Iran's farmers account for more than 90% of water usage and have been repeatedly encouraged to accelerate crop and stock production to feed a population starved by government ineptitude and mismanagement. Faced with dwindling water supplies, Iran's farmers have been forced to bore deeper wells into the depleting groundwater resources to irrigate their crops and water their livestock. It is reckoned that the number of wells has multiplied more than thirteen times since the 1979 revolution, with most of them illegal and draining far more water than can be sustainably maintained.

Figure 35 - Farmers of Varzaneh protest for their right to water.

Now renewable water resources, which were estimated at around 135 billion cubic meters in 1979, have fallen to 80 billion cubic meters, with experts predicting that water shortages may force up to 70% of Iranians or 58 million people, to move to other parts of Iran, or eventually to flee the country altogether if something is not done to resolve the crisis in the next 20 to 30 years.

Ongoing extreme summer heat and lack of rainfall has caused an extended drought, creating catastrophic water shortages and desertification, particularly in Khuzestan province in the southwest of the country. The theocratic regime has reacted in its usual brutal fashion, ordering a vicious crackdown on large-scale street protests that have resulted in the death of at least ten young demonstrators and the injury of many others. This has enraged the thirsty and frustrated crowds, who have seen their running water dry up almost entirely, leading to angry and often violent strikes, sit-ins and uprisings. Thousands of largely Iranian Arab citizens can be heard in videos chanting in Arabic: "We are thirsty!" and "We want the regime to fall!" Iranian police and IRGC personnel have used teargas, shrapnel and live ammunition to disperse the protesters. According to the Iranian Department of Water and Sewerage, at least 110 Iranian cities have experienced regular water cuts during the summer of 2022, although resistance units of the main democratic opposition group, the PMOI/MEK state that more than 200 towns and cities have been seriously affected. They claim that there are some cities in Khuzestan that literally have no running water.

Water levels in the Karkeh River in Khuzestan, one of the legendary four great biblical rivers of the Garden of Eden, have fallen dangerously low due to environmental damage and mismanagement. The situation has been exacerbated by water shortages in other semi-arid Iranian provinces like Isfahan, where irrigation canals have diverted water from major river systems to supply heavy industry. The resulting severe water shortages have caused running water from rivers and lakes to become excessively salty, impacting negatively on crop and livestock production. It is claimed that already over 1.2 million date palms, a crucial income source for farmers in Khuzestan, have died of drought. The protests in Khuzestan ignited further mass demonstrations in Tehran, where 9 million city inhabitants reached breaking point with the clerical regime. Videos on social media showed women outside a Tehran metro station chanting "Down with the Islamic Republic" in solidarity with the Khuzestan protesters. Similar mass protests erupted in towns and cities across Iran and eventually merged into the nationwide uprising now affecting the entire country. In an anti-regime protest in Tabriz, in Azerbaijan Province in north-western Iran, demonstrators were filmed chanting "Azerbaijanis, Kurds, Persians united" and "Azeris are awakened, support Khuzestan."

Deforestation, which had been going on since 1900 when Iran enjoyed extensive forest-cover, accelerated after the mullahs came to power in the 1979 revolution. Nineteen million acres of trees in 1900, has shrunk to less than eleven million acres today. This has coincided with a sharp reduction in annual rainfall, caused partly due to deforestation and environmental degradation and partly to climate change, leading to desertification and water shortages. Alarmingly, Iran now ranks fourth in the World Resources Institute's list of the countries at the greatest risk of exhausting their water supply. While dozens were killed by torrential rainstorms and floods in 2022, thousands more suffer from drought and water scarcity in other parts of Iran, where lakes, rivers and aquifers have dried up.

The mullahs' response to the growing economic crisis has devastated Iran's fragile environment. Determined to achieve self-sufficiency in agriculture and several other sectors, the theocratic regime ordered the felling of forests and draining of reservoirs, to create more available land for growing crops. The results were predictable, with environmental degradation accelerating and poverty and deprivation growing exponentially. Refusing to accept responsibility for these self-inflicted disasters, the mullahs turned their fury onto Iran's dwindling community of environmentalists, arresting some of them on trumped-up spying charges. One environmentalist even died under mysterious circumstances in prison, while others fled abroad in fear for their lives.

It is this sort of prevailing paranoia in Iran that has hounded out those who could have helped the situation and forced a brain drain that has seen most of Iran's best environmental scientists flee the country. As Iran creeps steadily closer towards ecological meltdown, environmental concerns have figured prominently in protests, particularly in regions populated by ethnic minorities like the Azeris and Iranian Arabs. The mullahs have reacted with typical viciousness, shooting dead unarmed protesters and arresting hundreds of others. But as water and food shortages grow, the Iranian population is becoming increasingly aware of the fact that the government is no longer capable of delivering basic public goods and services. The tipping point has been reached. Without adequate supplies of food and water, over 80 million enraged Iranians will quickly lose their fear of batons and bullets.

It was against this background that it was announced that the president of Iran – Ebrahim Raisi – the Butcher of Tehran – intended to attend the international climate change summit meeting in Glasgow called COP 26 in November 2021. Immediately, a formal request was sent to the Chief Constable of Scotland Police - Iain Livingstone, calling on him to mount a criminal investigation under universal jurisdiction, into accusations of genocide and crimes against humanity by Raisi. Universal jurisdiction allows a state to claim criminal jurisdiction over an accused person regardless of where the alleged crime was committed and regardless of the accused's nationality, country, or residence. Prosecutions under universal jurisdiction are always for the most serious crimes. A 111-page dossier was submitted to the Chief Constable of Police Scotland, signed by five direct victims or relatives of victims who suffered torture, human rights abuse and in many cases extra-judicial execution, at the hands of or under the command of Ebrahim Raisi.

At a press conference on Wednesday 13th October 2021, in the Village Hotel, Glasgow, some of the plaintiffs and signatories to the formal complaint outlined their reason for seeking the prosecution of Ebrahim Raisi by Police Scotland, in advance of the COP26 Climate Change Summit in Glasgow, to which the Iranian president had been invited. The plaintiffs demanded if he set foot in Scotland he should be arrested. The plaintiffs, all of whom had British-Iranian dual nationality, outlined some of the harrowing details of the suffering they or their relatives or cellmates had endured at the hands of Raisi.

Raisi is on the US sanctions list for serial human rights violations. Amnesty International and Human Rights Watch have both called for his indictment for human rights violations and crimes against humanity. Agnès Callamard, the Secretary General of Amnesty International, called for Raisi to be investigated for crimes against humanity and for his involvement in murder, enforced disappearance and torture. In his report of 16 July 2021 to the UN General Assembly, on human rights in Iran, Professor Javaid Rehman raised concerns regarding the destruction of evidence of the extrajudicial executions that took place in 1988. On 4 August 2021, the UN working Group on Enforced Disappearances in a report to the UN Human Rights Council, called for an "international investigation" into the 1988 massacre, stating that "The Working Group reiterates the concerns expressed about the ongoing concealment of burial sites across the country. The Working Group recalls that an enforced disappearance continues until the fate and whereabouts of the individuals concerned are established."

The UN Secretary-General - António Guterres, has now issued a damning report on the grave human rights violations that have occurred in Iran in which he expresses his concern over impunity from past violations such as the 1988 massacre of political prisoners. The UN Secretary-General has accused the Iranian regime of "destroying evidence of the execution of political dissidents at that time (1988) and the harassment and criminal prosecution of families of victims calling for truth and accountability."

In a covering letter to Chief Constable Livingstone of Police Scotland, the plaintiffs stated that they, or their relatives or cellmates, were "subjected to torture and extra-judicial executions on a large scale". In their testimonies, they described how in the summer of 1988, they were taken to Gohardasht Prison, where, in a two or three-minute hearing, they were confronted by Raisi, in his role as a public prosecutor and asked if they continued to support the PMOI/MEK. If they answered "Yes" they and hundreds of others were lined up in a corridor, sometimes for hours, then taken in groups into an execution chamber where they were forced to watch other prisoners being hanged, before being executed themselves. One survived to provide testimony because he had fainted at the sight of his fellow prisoners being hanged.

When Ebrahim Raisi, the president of Iran, heard that a formal request had been made to the Metropolitan Police and the Scottish Police, to have him arrested for crimes against humanity and genocide if he attempted to attend the COP26 Climate Summit in Glasgow, he quickly chickened out. Raisi realized that, unlike his predecessors, he is unable to travel freely to the West, or indeed to any civilized nation, due to his pariah status as the 'Butcher of Tehran'. Raisi's humiliating climbdown signalled that he had woken up to the fact that as president, he had inherited a poisoned chalice. He is the zombie president of a dying regime. The Iranian economy has collapsed due to corruption and incompetence. There is mass unemployment, plummeting household incomes and stagflation. In a disastrous attempt to repair the damage, the theocratic regime has attempted to manipulate the foreign-exchange rate, drained resources from the central bank, sold state-owned companies and factories and plundered the stock market. They even began to deal in bitcoins.

Raisi has tried to hide his embarrassment by claiming that he had never been invited to attend COP26 in Glasgow. That lie was quickly exposed by the fact that a team from Iran actually attended the summit. Of course, Raisi wanted to come himself to rub shoulders with world leaders who were in Scotland. But he knew that the UN, the Swiss Federal Court, the Courts in Sweden, Amnesty International, Human Rights Watch and a list of other international organisations, governments and legislatures were and still are, actively discussing his involvement in the 1988 massacre. He knows they are also examining his role in the murder of 1,500 young protesters during the nationwide uprising in Iran in

November 2019. He knows they are investigating the hundreds of executions that took place while he was head of the judiciary, executions that are accelerating now that he is president, as he attempts to frighten the restive population into servility. There must be no impunity for mass murderers like Raisi. Indeed, the news in 2021 that the International Criminal Court in the Hague (ICC) had launched a full probe into Rodrigo Duterte, at that time the president of the Philippines, for his involvement in crimes against humanity and murder, sent shockwaves to Tehran. Duterte's extra-judicial killings in his so-called 'war on drugs' could lead to his indictment, arrest and appearance in the ICC, paving the way for a similar indictment against Raisi.

In any case, it was simply a joke that the mullahs' regime should pretend that they had the slightest interest in COP26. The head of the regime's Environmental Protection Agency recently said that an enemy could never have damaged Iran's natural resources and environment the way the mullahs have. The regime's rank incompetence, venal corruption and voracious profiteering have increased the risk and the incidence of natural disasters in Iran. The devastating floods, raging forest fires, toxic air pollution, uncontrolled desertification and grave water shortages have all pushed the Iranian environment to the edge of destruction. The IRGC are playing a key role in this environmental catastrophe thanks to their institutionalized corruption and destructive policies.

In the last 5 years alone, 60,000 hectares of the country's forests have been destroyed due to fire, pests, disease, dams, road building, other construction activities and timber smuggling, much of it under the control of the IRGC. Forest fires are destroying another 12,000 hectares every year. Rapid desertification, due to the IRGC's reckless dam-building programme, has caused Iran to lose more than two-thirds of its agricultural land through drought and subsidence. Sand and dust storms now wreck crops. Air pollution is so severe in Tehran and most large cities that schools, businesses and government offices must be regularly closed because of dangerously high levels of toxins. Tehran and other large Iranian cities are among the most polluted cities of the world.

As delegates at COP26 in Glasgow discussed the global climate emergency, 80 million Iranians were already suffering the consequences of environmental depredation at the hands of the theocratic regime. During its 4 decades in power, the mullahs not only slaughtered the Iranian people, violated human rights and spread terror around the world, they also caused irreversible destruction to the Iranian environment. The answer to the environmental crisis in Iran, as well as the answer to the economic crisis, the answer to the social crisis and the answer to the security crisis across the Middle East and worldwide, is the downfall of the mullahs' totalitarian regime.

Chapter Eighteen

THE DOOR IS CLOSING FOR THE MULLAHS

The door of history is closing on the mullahs' theocratic regime. Today the Iranian regime faces European justice. This may be a concept difficult to understand for a fascist tyranny that uses intimidation, torture, and execution as the mainstays of its oppression. In 2022 the mullahs saw a court in Belgium extend the prison terms of the three co-conspirators who together with the Iranian diplomat Assadollah Assadi, attempted to bomb a mass opposition rally near Paris in 2018. All of them will spend decades in jail for acts of terrorism. Now Hamid Noury, an agent of the regime, has joined the ranks of terrorist murderers and executioners held to account by European courts.[83]

In their case against Noury, under universal jurisdiction, the Swedish judiciary cited evidence that a large number of PMOI/MEK prisoners were executed between 30 July and 16 August 1988 in the Gohardasht prison in Karaj, Iran, where he was assistant to the deputy prosecutor. The indictment stated that Noury was "suspected of participating, together with other perpetrators, in these mass executions and, as such, intentionally taking the lives of a large number of prisoners, who sympathised with the Mojahedin and, additionally, of subjecting prisoners to severe suffering which is deemed torture and inhuman treatment." He was found guilty of these heinous crimes.

The Swedish prosecutors gathered extensive evidence from witnesses and survivors of the 1988 massacre. Their testaments were horrifying. Witness after witness recounted how Noury helped with

---

[83] Tanner, Jari. "Sweden prosecutes Iranian man for 1980s war crimes at prison," Associated Press, July 27, 2021.

the selection of PMOI/MEK prisoners who were brought before a summary court where they were asked simply if they still supported the Mojahedin. If, during an arbitrary three-minute hearing, they answered 'yes', they were immediately blindfolded and led to the so-called 'death corridor' by Noury, where he would order them to stand in line, sometimes for hours, before escorting them to the execution chamber before being executed themselves. Nouri often attended and participated in the hanging of prisoners. One witness survived to provide testimony because he had fainted at the sight of his fellow prisoners being hanged.

Noury was arrested at Stockholm's Arlanda Airport on 9th November 2019. He had been warned by friends that he risked arrest if he travelled to Sweden, but he brazenly boasted that he spent ten days in Sweden every year and wasn't worried. There is a strong suggestion that the mullahs had actively planned his arrest and had hoped to subvert his trial by introducing undercover agents working for the regime as fake witnesses, in the belief that they could win Noury's acquittal and discredit the PMOI/MEK. Their conspiracy backfired spectacularly.

Figure 36 - Hamid Noury, convicted of involvement in 1988 Massacre

In an unprecedented move, the Swedish Court even relocated to Durrës Province in Albania for ten days to hear evidence from key witnesses to the killings who now live in Ashraf 3, headquarters of more than 3,000 PMOI/MEK supporters in Albania. Six Swedish judges, two prosecutors and the plaintiff's lawyer, heard evidence from the witnesses in Albania from 10th to 19th November 2021, while Noury and his lawyers participated via video conference from Sweden.[84]

The guilty verdict in Sweden and the life sentence on Noury was a direct embarrassment to Iran's executioner president Ebrahim Raisi. Noury was one of Raisi's functionaries and even described how on one occasion he brought a box of pastries to Raisi who proceeded to gorge himself on the delicacies while sentencing young men and women to be hanged. The Swedish verdict proved that under universal jurisdiction Raisi himself and the other criminal members of the hierarchy in the mullahs' regime could all be prosecuted and held to account for their crimes if they ever dare to set foot in any civilized country.

Figure 37 - Crowds welcome the life sentence for Hamid Noury in Stockholm

In retaliation for a series of setbacks in the European courts, the fundamentalist Iranian regime instigated a series of terrorist threats to attack an annual rally of anti-regime dissidents and their

[84] "Iranian ex-official's trial resumes in Albania," AFP, November 10, 2021.

supporters in Albania, leading to the postponement of the event on security grounds. The rally was scheduled to take place over the weekend of 23 and 24 July 2022 in Ashraf 3, headquarters of the PMOI/MEK.[85]

The Albanian government called for the last-minute postponement of the event on Friday 22 July, due to "terrorist threats and conspiracies." Ashraf 3, in Durres, is 30 kilometres (19 miles) west of Albania's capital, Tirana, and is home to over 3,000 members of the main Iranian democratic opposition movement. The 'Free Iran World Summit 2022' was due to be attended by dozens of US Senators, Congressmen, world leaders and distinguished international politicians and personalities, many of whom had already arrived in Tirana when news of the postponement was announced.

The theocratic regime in Tehran was infuriated by the jailing in Sweden on 14 July of Hamid Noury. Noury's life sentence followed the 20-year jail-term imposed in Belgium last year on Assadollah Assadi. As the full impact of European justice came home to roost in Tehran, the mullahs reacted in their normal way, by plotting lethal terror attacks on the planned mass gathering in Albania, causing its last-minute postponement. In a separate move they also announced the apparent arrest of several spies, allegedly working for Mossad. The Iranian Ministry of Intelligence and Security (MOIS) claimed that the "Israeli spies" had been caught after crossing the border from Iraqi Kurdistan, apparently carrying weapons, explosives, and communication equipment. The MOIS has so far failed to provide the names or number of those seized.

Alarmed that Europe faced a fuel crisis during the winter of 2022, due to the severance of oil and gas supplies from Russia, following the war in Ukraine, EU political leaders desperately sought ways of establishing new energy sources. The theocratic regime in Tehran demanded the lifting of all sanctions as a pre-condition for

---

[85] "Albania, host of Iranian dissident camp, expels two Iranian diplomats," Reuters, January 15, 2020.

resurrecting the nuclear deal and recommencing gas and oil supplies to the West. The EU's main appeasers, including Josep Borrell, the European Union's High Representative for Foreign Affairs & Security and Charles Michel, President of the European Council and former Prime Minister of Belgium, bent over backwards to appease the mullahs, oblivious to the litany of bomb plots, assassinations and terrorist attacks planned and carried out by the clerical regime's agents and so-called diplomats. The threats and conspiracies uncovered in Albania should have sounded the alarm, but kick-starting oil and gas supplies seem to take precedence over the safety and protection from terrorist attacks of European citizens.

Meanwhile, despite the regime's crackdown, the PMOI/MEK's resistance units continued to expand across the country. During Raisi's term, these resistance units have carried out at least 2,350 acts of resistance against the regime symbols of repression in various towns, 85% percent of them successfully.[86] During a recent gathering of the NCRI, video clips of some 5,000 Resistance Units voicing support and expressing their commitment to a free and democratic Iran were displayed, showing a five-fold increase in the number of the Resistance Units sending messages of support relative to last year.[87] The PMOI/MEK Resistance Units are now playing a key role in the nationwide revolution in Iran.

---

[86] "Iran: Ebrahim Raisi's Presidency, One Year On," NCRI, August 3, 2022.

[87] "The Next Iranian Revolution Is Being Shaped by The MEK Resistance Units," NCRI, August 9, 2022.

Chapter Nineteen

THE APEX APPEASERS

EU attempts to appease the Iranian regime reached their apex with the approval in July 2022 of a Belgium-Iran Treaty to enable the transfer of prisoners. It was an almost unbelievable scandal. It was agreed that terrorist prisoners of Iranian nationality in Belgium and prisoners of Belgian nationality held hostage in Iran, would be exchanged and purportedly allowed to serve their prison sentences in their respective home countries. But in a grovelling act of appeasement to the criminal Iranian regime, the treaty also allowed amnesty to be granted to the exchanged prisoners.

The intention of the Treaty, without doubt, was the release from prison of the Iranian terrorist diplomat, Assadollah Assadi, and his three co-conspirators. The EU appeasers clearly hoped that the agreement would improve their chances of resurrecting the deeply flawed JCPOA nuclear deal, implemented by Obama in 2015 and unilaterally abandoned by Trump in 2018. Since that time, the EU appeasers had tried desperately to resurrect the zombie deal, but the mullahs refused to cooperate unless sanctions were lifted, enabling them to kick-start their crumbling economy. The EU's main appeasers saw this as a prime way of acquiring Iranian oil and gas, to fill the vacuum left by the Russian war in Ukraine. It was a classic act of appeasement and a classic betrayal of the core principles of European justice.

The release from prison in Belgium of Iran's convicted terrorists was certain to send the clearest signal to the Iranian regime that they could continue to use their embassies and diplomats in Europe to conduct terrorist attacks with impunity. Indeed, the agreement encouraged them to take further European hostages to hold as bargaining chips for future prisoner exchanges.

If the EU's appeasers allow these killers and perpetrators of evil to escape the judgement of our courts and to be freed, the founding principles of European justice will be forever shattered. The theocratic regime's terrorists must he held to account and must face the justice of our courts. At midnight on July 20, 2022, immediately after the Belgian Parliament's adoption of the shameful treaty calling for a prisoner exchange between Belgium and the Iranian regime, Mrs. Rajavi, former Algerian Prime Minister Sid Ahmed Ghazali, former Italian Foreign Minister Giulio Terzi, former Colombian presidential candidate Ingrid Betancourt, Senator Robert Torricelli, former White House director for public liaison Linda Chavez, former UNAMI human rights office chief Tahar Boumedra, NCRI Foreign Affairs Committee Chairman Mohammad Mohaddessin, NCRI Judiciary Committee Chairman Dr. Sanabargh Zahedi, Javad Dabiran, Deputy NCRI Representative in Germany, and Farzin Hashemi, NCRI Representative in the international courts, submitted an urgent request to prevent Assadi's repatriation to Iran. Subsequently, the Court of Appeal ruled for a substantive re-consideration of the case. The Iranian opposition and its supporters do not intend to allow European justice to be subverted by such shameful treaties as the one agreed by the Belgian parliament.

In a desperate attempt to secure Assadi's release, the mullahs' regime arrested the Belgian humanitarian aid worker Olivier Vandecasteele, charging him with spying on Iran, cooperating with the United States against Iran, currency smuggling and money laundering. He was sentenced initially in December 2022 to 28 years imprisonment on these fabricated charges. When this blatant exercise in blackmail and hostage-taking failed to achieve the terrorist Assadi's repatriation, Iran's Supreme Leader, the elderly and increasingly deranged Ayatollah Ali Khamenei, in January 2023, ordered his judiciary to increase Vandecasteele's sentence to 40 years jail, together with 74 lashes and a $1 million fine.

The Belgian government should not bend to this dirty blackmail. They should announce that they will indict Khamenei for human rights abuse and crimes against humanity and try him in the international courts of justice, in absentia, if Vandecasteele is lashed. While there is understandably great sympathy for Mr Vandecasteele and his family and friends, there should be no question of negotiating a prisoner exchange with the mullahs. To do so would simply encourage further hostage taking and would provide impunity for the regime's perpetrators of any future deadly terrorist attacks in Europe. The only certain way to secure Mr Vandecasteele's freedom is to support the Iranian population in their bid to overthrow the mullahs' fascist dictatorship.

Chapter Twenty

DEMONIZING THE OPPOSITION

A French daily newspaper, Libération, founded by the famous philosopher Jean-Paul Sartre in 1973, published an article on 26th November 2021 trotting out the Iranian regime's greatest hits about the PMOI/MEK, calling them an "Islamic-Marxist group" who "sided with Saddam Hussein" that has "been on the lists of terrorist organizations in the United States and in Europe for years." All lies and all tired and weary propaganda, fed into the system by Iran's Ministry of Intelligence and Security (MOIS), a sinister KGB-style organization that is itself on the US and EU terrorist lists. The article was typical of the repeated attempts by the theocratic regime to demonize the main democratic opposition PMOI/MEK.

Fake News has even been exposed at Der Spiegel, the popular and previously widely respected German news magazine, with a weekly circulation of just under one million readers. In late 2018, Der Spiegel's star reporter, the freelancer Claas Relotius, admitted that he made up and invented stories that won him dozens of top awards for journalism and saw him acclaimed as journalist of the year by CNN in 2014.[88] Relotius also wrote investigative articles for Die Welt, Die Zeit and for some US and British newspapers. The scandal led to a huge outpouring of anguish by the various journals who used Relotius' work, with many leading journalists stating that he had undermined the credibility of the profession.

The unfolding scandal in Germany should have rung alarm bells in Britain, where fake news has regularly begun to make inroads into media outlets that were once respected for their integrity. Left-wing press like the Guardian and Channel 4 News have both published

---

[88] " Claas Relotius: Der Spiegel reporter wrote fake stories 'on a grand scale'," CNN, December 21, 2018.

outrageous stories traducing the PMOI/MEK and Iranian refugees currently residing at Ashraf 3 in Albania. The formerly tiny Iranian embassy in Albania was transformed into one of the Iranian regime's largest embassies in the Balkans. In early 2016, as the PMOI/MEK dissidents were being transferred to Albania in groups, Tehran sent a new ambassador, Gholam Hossein Mohammadinia, to Albania. Mohammadinia was a former high-ranking intelligence MOIS official and was also a member of the Iranian nuclear negotiating team before accepting his appointment in Albania. His main mandate in Tirana was to continue to implement the regime's malign plots against the PMOI. The embassy became the focus of an expanding nest of 25 intelligence agents and spies.

In late 2017, another senior intelligence official, Mostafa Roudaki, joined him as First Secretary. He became the Iranian Intelligence Ministry's (MOIS) station chief in Albania. He was previously head of the Iranian regime's intelligence station in Austria and had been coordinating surveillance and terrorist activities against the PMOI/MEK in Europe. He was replaced in Austria by Assadollah Assadi, the 'so-called' diplomat, who was arrested in Germany in July 2018 for plotting a terrorist bomb outrage. Prior to that in March 2018 a terrorist plot against a New Year celebration gathering of the PMOI/MEK members in Tirana was foiled and when the finger of blame was pointed at Iran's ambassador to Albania, Gholam Hossein Mohammadinia and his First Secretary Mostafa Roudaki, the two were expelled from the country by Albania's Prime Minister Edi Rama in December 2018, on the grounds that they posed a threat to national security.[89]

Prime Minister Rama received a letter of praise and congratulations from President Trump on 14th December 2018, saying "thank you for your steadfast decision to stand up to Iran to counter its destabilization activities and efforts to silence dissidents around the globe. The leadership you have shown by expelling Iran's ambassador to your country exemplifies our joint efforts to show

---

[89] "Albania expels Iranian diplomats on national security grounds," Reuters, December 19, 2018.

the Iranian government that its terrorist activities in Europe and around the world will have severe consequences."

But prior to these expulsions the demonization campaign against the PMOI/MEK had begun. For this purpose, the mullahs focused their attention on elements of the Western media, manipulating their anti-Trump, anti-American, anti-Saudi Arabian agenda to encompass a smear campaign against the PMOI/MEK. As part of this policy the Iranian regime set up official or unofficial intelligence and surveillance stations in the Balkans. Massoud Khodabandeh and his wife, Anne Singleton, two well-known UK-based MOIS agents, identified as such in a Library of Congress and Pentagon Report,[90] were flown to Tirana several times. In October 2018, when Twitter revealed a large number of tweets and re-tweets posted by the MOIS and the IRGC, it became clear that many of the regime's Twitter accounts quoted Khodabandeh and Singleton. The MOIS had clearly instructed these two agents to focus all their resources on the PMOI/MEK presence in Albania.

Sure enough, in due course, some gullible Western journalists were spotted prowling around the new compound being constructed by the Ashrafis near the town of Manza, in the Albanian province of Durres. Soon, both Channel 4 News and the Guardian ran smear stories targeting the Iranian refugees in Albania, likening them to a cult, living in a tightly secured military compound. One article even alleged that they had kidnapped and murdered some of their own supporters. The claims were preposterous and easily disproved. The compound in Manza employed more than 600 local Albanians on a daily basis. Thousands of relatives of the refugees who had been prevented from seeing them in Iraq for years, had flown to Albania and visited the camp. Lawyers, politicians and human rights activists were and still are regular visitors to Ashraf 3. But none of this was reported by Channel 4 News and the Guardian. Indeed, the fact that their reports appeared almost word for word in a website created by the Iranian agents Khodabandeh and Singleton

---

[90] "Iran's Ministry of Intelligence and Security: A Profile," A report prepared by the Federal Research Division, Library of Congress, December 2012.

three weeks before being published in the UK, exposed the sinister source of the prejudicial fake news.

Alerted to the likelihood of these fake articles appearing, many prominent politicians wrote to Channel 4 News and the Guardian warning them that they would be publishing fake news and playing into the hands of the mullahs and their terrorist and repressive regime. The warnings were ignored. The clear assumption must be that the policy of appeasing the mullahs has found a much deeper well of sympathy in some parts of the European media than previously thought. Editorial policy that condones the publication of fake news of this magnitude not only undermines the integrity of journalism, as Der Spiegel was forced to admit, it drives a stake into the heart of the Iranian people, whose nationwide protests against the mullah's fascist regime have now exploded into a full-scale revolution.

Weaker than at any time since the 1979 revolution, the Iranian regime is like a dangerous, wounded animal, lashing out to preserve its existence. Its economy broken and reeling from the twin blows of courts in Belgium and Sweden sentencing its agents to long terms of imprisonment for terrorist offences and crimes against humanity, the mullahs are in meltdown. Realizing in July 2022 that the PMOI/MEK was about to stage an international rally at Ashraf 3, their headquarters-in-exile in Albania, Khamenei and Raisi dispatched a team of trained assassins from the regime's Ministry of Intelligence and Security (MOIS) and its terrorist Quds Force, to carry out a large-scale attack on the convention. Fortunately, Albania's intelligence service and their international partners from the USA, intercepted several coded messages about the planned attack and the Albanian government advised the summit should be postponed on security grounds.

Four of the regime's agents were stopped from entering Albania at the international airport in Tirana. All four were expelled. Earlier in July, the Albanian authorities had raided the homes of 11 MOIS agents, confiscating their computers and cell phones and interrogating them for ten hours. The crackdown on the theocratic regime's terrorists in Albania followed the expulsion of the Iranian Ambassador and First Secretary in December 2018, by Albania's prime minister Edi Rama. They were listed as personae non grate for endangering the security of the state by plotting bomb outrages from within the Iranian embassy. It also followed the sentencing to 20 years imprisonment in Belgium of the Iranian diplomat - Assadollah Assadi, and his three co-conspirators, for plotting a bomb attack on another major opposition rally in Paris in June 2018. When police searched Assadi's car, they discovered a notebook recording the addresses and contact details of 289 MOIS agents and mercenaries, many of them listed as official Iranian refugees. One hundred and forty-four of them live in Germany.

Frustrated at their inability to cause terrorist carnage in Albania, the mullahs resorted to their traditional ploy, demonizing the opposition. The MOIS maintains a bank of helpful journalists and lobbyists in the West that it unleashes at times of crisis to demonize the PMOI/MEK with outrageous accusations and denunciations. The Western media who accept clandestine payments or other inducements from the mullahs' fascist regime to publish such fabrications should hang their heads in shame, but sadly many well-known newspapers and TV channels still do. It is a sad fact that there are still journalists today who ignore the truth, preferring instead to abuse, traduce and vilify the men and women of the PMOI/MEK who have given up their professional careers and family lives and often even life itself, to devote themselves to the cause of ending oppression and tyranny in Iran.

The demonization machinery is still at work, and it seems as if the propaganda campaign is designed, not to fool the Iranian people, but the Western media, who often report regime talking points without even investigating them. The MOIS oversees spreading false rumours and fake news against the PMOI/MEK and it does so by employing 'disinformation agents' who are recruited from the opposite ends of the spectrum. Some had purposely infiltrated the PMOI/MEK to gain insider information before leaving, while others were former members of the PMOI/MEK who either departed of their own accord or were expelled from the organization. Those who were expelled were then pressured into joining Iran's intelligence agency through bribery and coercion, with their family members being threatened with imprisonment if the former PMOI/MEK members refused to cooperate.

In Albania, the renewed demonization campaign in the summer of 2022 took the form of a series of crude and unsophisticated allegations of theft, drug trafficking and money-laundering, libelled against named PMOI/MEK individuals from Ashraf 3. Faked official documents, supposedly signed by the public prosecutor and senior police officers in Tirana, were distributed to the media, but were quickly exposed as fraudulent by the Albanian authorities. Albania's intelligence services raided a café in Tirana which had become a known meeting place for PMOI/MEK dropouts from Ashraf 3, who were subsequently recruited by the MOIS. The café in Tirana was also the address of the ASILA Association, an 'NGO' financed by the Iranian regime. A known MOIS agent called Hassan Heyrani, who was kicked out of the PMOI/MEK in Ashraf 3, had been the source of several outlandish press reports following media interviews with Western journalists in the same café. One of the agents frequenting the café and active in Albania was Bijan Pooladrag, claiming to be a "former member of the PMOI". He was arrested and tried for espionage for the Iranian regime and was convicted and sentenced to 10 years in prison.

The exposure of attempts by the Iranian regime to commit a terrorist outrage in Albania should have been a wake-up call for Western appeasers who continue to mollify the mullahs. The theocratic regime's mercenaries in Europe who have posed deceptively as refugees, should have their passports and EU citizenship revoked. Known agents from the MOIS and Quds Force should be arrested, prosecuted and expelled and Iran's network of embassies, which they use as bomb factories and terrorist cells, should be closed down and their so-called diplomats banished. When this evil dictatorship in toppled, history will record the names of those journalists who played this dishonest game in a rollcall of shame. Jean-Paul Sartre said: "Every word has consequences. Every silence, too."

Following the very successful Free Iran World Summit-2021, the regime was greatly angered, particularly by the fact that many of the high-level speakers called for the regime and its newly appointed president, Ebrahim Raisi, to be held accountable for human rights violations and crimes against humanity. Thus, in a predictable response, the regime employed its disinformation machinery to discredit the NCRI and the PMOI/MEK. Iranian state media produced over 300 movies and TV shows between 2015 and 2016 that were designed to demonize the MEK, while in 2016 alone the regime published 14 different books for the same purpose. The regime has at least 13 websites, a monthly magazine, and countless social media accounts that perpetuate this disinformation campaign year-round.

Iran's rulers have made all these efforts to somehow discredit its viable democratic alternative because of its utter fear of the PMOI/MEK potential in leading the struggle for freedom in Iran. This was shown back in 1981 when the group led a 500,000-strong peaceful anti-regime march in Tehran that was brutally crushed by regime agents who used live ammunition on protesters, killing hundreds. This failed to quash the group, so the regime issued a crackdown, which culminated in the 1988 massacre of 30,000 political prisoners, mainly PMOI/MEK members and supporters. Even this could not stop support for the group, so the propaganda machine was born, and the resistance units have grown exponentially in towns and cities across Iran.

The recruitment process of the MOIS came to light in 2000 when Jamshid Tafrishi, a former MOIS agent, defected and made his experiences public. As a disinformation agent, he had pretended to be an opponent of the Iranian regime, all the while he was completing assignments on behalf of the MOIS. His activities involved distributing false information to foreign governments and the media and giving lectures on the 'imprisonment, torture, and harassment of former MEK members. He defected from the service in 2000 after becoming disillusioned with their operations and, a year later, confessed to the US Court of Appeals that he had been working as an agent for the MOIS. In the affidavit he submitted to the court, he stated: "From 1995 to 1999, I received a total of $72,000 from the MOIS as payment for my work on their behalf."

The most recent example of the recruited disinformation agent is Hadi Sani-Khani, who is a former operative of the MOIS residing in Albania. In a letter to the United Nations Secretary-General in February 2021, he unveiled a new and shocking campaign of demonization as well as espionage and terrorism against the PMOI/MEK and emphasized that he was prepared to testify and prove his revelations with ample documents and evidence before any court or impartial authority.

Figure 38 - MOIS Agents Massoud Khodabandeh and his British wife Anne Singleton

'Iran-Interlink' is one of the most active websites launched by the MOIS in Farsi and English, with the sole objective of demonizing the PMOI/MEK. The directors of this website are Massoud Khodabandeh and his British wife Anne Singleton.

The US Pentagon & the Library of Congress formally exposed Anne Singleton as an Iranian spy in an official report published in January 2013. The report entitled: 'Iran's Ministry of Intelligence and

Security: a profile' was based on exhaustive research undertaken by the Pentagon and the US Federal Research Division, Library of Congress. It made striking revelations about the extent of activities by the Iranian Ministry of Intelligence and Security (MOIS) against dissidents and in particular efforts to discredit the main opposition People's Mojahedin Organisation of Iran (PMOI/MEK). The report identified two MOIS agents operating with Iran and explained how they had been recruited and trained by the MOIS in Tehran to run a demonization campaign, including launching a PMOI-defamatory website: www.iran-interlink.org.[91]

The Pentagon report stated: "The recruitment of a British subject, Anne Singleton, and her Iranian husband, Massoud Khodabandeh, provides a relevant example of how MOIS coerces non-Iranians to cooperate. She worked with the MEK in the late 1980s. Massoud Khodabandeh and his brother Ibrahim were both members of the MEK at the time. In 1996 Massoud Khodabandeh decided to leave the organisation. Later, he married Anne Singleton. Soon after their marriage, MOIS forced them to cooperate by threatening to confiscate Khodabandeh's mother's extensive property in Tehran. Singleton and Khodabandeh then agreed to work for MOIS and spy on the MEK.

Alarmingly, the Pentagon report also showed that Iran's known agents had enjoyed freedom of activity in Europe for years. The report made it clear that the Quds Force and the Islamic Revolutionary Guards Corps, together with the MOIS who control their activities, were involved in conspiracies to murder citizens and residents of the EU. Similar reports have been made by some European Intelligence Services. The German Interior Ministry's Annual Report in 2013 on the Protection of the Constitution stated: "1.2 Target areas and focus of information gathering. Priority task of the Iranian intelligence service apparatus is espionage and to combat opposition movements at home and abroad. Moreover, in the West, information from the fields of politics, economics and

---

[91] "Iran's Ministry of Intelligence and Security: A Profile," A report prepared by the Federal Research Division, Library of Congress, December 2012.

science to be procured. In the actions against Germany in particular from the MOIS, special focus is placed on the "People's Mojahedin of Iran Organization" (MEK) and its political arm, the "National Council of Resistance of Iran" (NCRI)."

And the Intelligence Services of the Netherlands, AIVD, 2012 report, page 37, states: "AIVD has realized that the government of Iran is constantly active against the resistance movement PMOI. The Iranian Ministry of Intelligence (MOIS) controls a network in Europe, which is also active in the Netherlands. Members of this network are former members of the PMOI who have been recruited by the MOIS. Their mission is to impose a negative impact on public opinion about the PMOI by lobbying, making publications and organizing anti-PMOI rallies. These people also gather information about the PMOI and its members for the MOIS. "

Chapter Twenty-One

IRAN'S MULLAHS TURN TO CYBERWARS

Following the introduction in 2018 of the final phase of tough US sanctions on Iran by Donald Trump, targeting oil exports, shipping and financial transactions, the clerical regime began to panic. Human Rights Monitor (HRM) reported an increase in executions, repression, and human rights abuse as the mullahs tried desperately to contain the growing unrest that saw nationwide protests continue for almost a year. HRM also reported arbitrary murders, deaths in custody, inhuman treatment, cruel punishments, appalling prison conditions and the continued persecution of religious minorities.

The US State Department published a 48-page report entitled "OUTLAW REGIME: A Chronicle of Iran's Destructive Activities." In a foreword, Secretary of State Mike Pompeo explained why President Trump had decided to withdraw from the nuclear deal and reimpose sanctions that had been lifted by Obama, calling it "a failed strategic bet that fell short of protecting the American people or our allies from the potential of an Iranian nuclear weapon."

In explosive comments, Mike Pompeo said: "The Islamic Republic of Iran is not a normal state. Normal states do not attack embassies and military installations in peacetime; fuel terrorist proxies and militias; serve as a sanctuary for terrorists; call for the destruction of Israel and threaten other countries; aid brutal dictators such as Syria's Bashar al-Assad; proliferate missile technology to dangerous proxies; conduct covert assassinations in other countries; and hold hostage citizens of foreign nations. Normal states do not support terrorism within their armed forces, as Iran has done with the Islamic Revolutionary Guard Corps (IRGC) and its Quds Force. Normal states do not abuse the international financial system and use commercial industry to fund and support terrorism. Normal states do not squander their own natural resources. Normal states do not violently suppress legitimate protests, jail their own citizens or those of other countries on specious crimes, engage in torture, and impose severe restrictions on basic freedoms."

Desperate to cling to power, the mullahs ramped up repression and turned to the exploitation of cyberwarfare to spread propaganda, influence events, shape foreign perceptions and counter perceived threats. The US State Department reported: "The Islamic Republic has developed its cyber capabilities with the intent to surveil and sabotage its adversaries, undermining international norms and threatening international stability."

A key target for the clerical regime's cyber-spies was, as always, the PMOI/MEK and NCRI. In particular, the regime instigated a determined campaign to strike out at Ashraf 3 in Albania, deploying cyberattacks to spread misinformation, fake news, and blatant fabrications, labelling the PMOI/MEK as a terrorist organization and claiming that their presence was a danger to Albania, Europe and the Middle East. It also utilized vast resources to procure the willing service of gullible Western journalists. While the Iranian regime's attempts to smear the PMOI/MEK lack credibility, these allegations often became the basis for future terrorist and criminal acts against the opposition. The Iranian Ministry of Intelligence (MOIS) likes to use the Western media to denigrate the PMOI in such a way that any subsequent terror attacks or assassinations targeting them receive little public sympathy.

In 2018, Twitter closed 770 accounts run by the Iranian regime, declaring them false accounts for government propaganda and for disseminating fake news and lies.[92] At the same time, Facebook, Instagram, and Google closed similar accounts related to the regime. On October 17, Twitter published content associated with these 770 accounts, amounting to 1,122,936 tweets, along with embedded photos and videos. Amongst these tweets were hundreds that had

---

[92] " Twitter found 10 million posts by Iran, Russia-backed accounts," CNBC, October 17, 2018.

been disseminated widely by Iran's MOIS in the days before the NCRI/PMOI annual rally in Paris in June, which always attracts a massive crowd of more than 100,000 expatriate Iranians opposed the mullahs' regime. Typical were tweets such as:

- We condemn that French government is hosting MKO #NoToMKO #TrumpSupportsTerrorism #GiulianiSupportsTerrorism #BanTerrorOrg https://t.co/ZFwc4vbJVd

- Mr president @EmmanuelMacron the so called #MEK group which has carried out numerous #terrorist activities in Iran, which has acted as mercenaries of Saddam Hussein and killed thousands of Iraqi Shiites and Iraqi Kurd is living freely in your country expel them please #BanTerrorOrg

The tactic of using social media to soften public opinion and sow seeds of doubt about the NCRI/PMOI as a prelude to a terrorist attack was highlighted when on 30th June that year German police arrested Assadollah Assadi, a diplomat from the Iranian Embassy in Vienna, and charged him with terrorist offences. He had conspired to bomb the rally in Paris.

Revelations that the Iranian regime has been peddling disinformation on social media in an attempt to influence the outcome of elections to the Scottish parliament in 2021, came as no surprise. Their fake posts and tweets on Facebook and Twitter which had been going on for at least twelve months and possibly had begun as far back as 2013, had been in support of Scottish independence and the fracturing of the UK. Like the Russians, the Iranian mullahs were keen to promote anything that might harm the West. Breaking up the UK was therefore a prime target for their cyber trolls, who targeted social media relentlessly with fake separatist material, graphics, memes, and cartoons, in an attempt to influence Scottish voters.

The Iranian regime's malign activities have been studied by the Henry Jackson Society, a transatlantic think tank. They reported that fake accounts and groups were set up by cyber-specialists from

Tehran to fool Scottish internet users. The Henry Jackson Society described it as an attempt by the mullahs' regime to "attack the constitutional integrity of the UK." With Nicola Sturgeon re-elected as Scotland's First Minister and an overall majority of MSPs in the Scottish Parliament who favoured independence, it looked as if the theocratic regime may have scored a hit with their disinformation campaign. The SNP may pause to reflect on the strange bedfellows they have accumulated during their endless separatist crusades, although they have stressed that they have never encouraged or endorsed such interference. Indeed, they claim to have worked "to counter the spread of disinformation." That may be the case, but the Scottish Government does have a track record in kowtowing to the mullahs.

There is little doubt that Tehran has put a great deal of effort into courting closer relationships with Scottish political leaders who favour independence. In December 2015, former First Minister Alex Salmond was one of a 6-person delegation who visited Tehran, meeting the Iranian Foreign Minister Javad Zarif and other representatives of the mullahs' regime, in an attempt to cement trade ties. The serious implications of Iranian interference in the Scottish elections triggered a robust response from James Cleverly MP, the then UK Minister for the Middle East and Africa, who said that he would raise Britain's concerns with international leaders at the G7 summit in Cornwall in June 2021. Mr Cleverly said that he would seek an agenda item at the summit meeting of foreign ministers, dealing with the Iranian regime's "destabilising behaviour, not just in the region but also more broadly."

The cyberwar activities of the theocratic regime are simply the tip of a dangerous iceberg. The mullahs' egregious abuse of human rights, their massacre of over 30,000 political prisoners in 1988, their murder of 1,500 protesters during a nationwide uprising in 2019 and their history of torture, brutality, injustice, and arbitrary executions, have turned Iran into a pariah state. In addition, their policy of aggressive expansionism across the Middle East and their role as the Godfather of international terror, with repeated cases of so-called 'diplomats' involved in terror plots in the West, have radically altered international attitudes to Tehran.

Perhaps anticipating the impending collapse of the regime, Iran's Foreign Minister Javad Zarif, in April 2021, was suspected of leaking a supposedly confidential and classified tape recording of an interview he gave, in which he openly criticized the IRGC. In the leaked tape, which caused a firestorm in Iran, Zarif could be heard to complain that he had to spend most of his time clearing up the diplomatic mess made by the IRGC. He claimed that he had no authority to take decisions and that all foreign policy was dictated by the IRGC acting on the direct instructions of Iran's Supreme Leader Ayatollah Ali Khamenei. Many Iran-watchers believed Zarif contrived to expose the tape as a future defence against indictments in the international courts for his involvement in cyberwars, terror plots and crimes against humanity. But his efforts backfired spectacularly, undermining his credibility as foreign minister, and highlighting his close involvement as a willing puppet in the Iranian regime's aggressive imperialist, expansionist and terrorist strategies.

The SNP government should beware that it doesn't find itself on the wrong side of history. There are growing signs that the fascist dictatorship ruling Iran is on its last legs, as 80 million Iranians clamour for change and long for the restoration of freedom, justice, and democracy. Scotland should always be on the side of the oppressed. Misguided support for the mullahs would be a grave error.

Chapter Twenty-Two

THE TIPPING POINT

Iran has reached an historic tipping point. There is mass unrest and seething hatred of the theocratic regime, combined with the collapsing economic situation and social repression. However, the regime is desperately clinging to power and is prepared to kill its own citizens indiscriminately to achieve that end. The people are unarmed, but they are steadily losing their fear of the oppressors and are resolute in their goal to overthrow the regime. They are uniting behind the leadership of the PMOI/MEK and their burgeoning resistance units knowing full well that the regime will not desist from its murderous course on its own will.

Unarmed young men and women are daily being beaten with iron bars, sprayed with tear gas, maimed with birdshot and killed by gunfire. As the nationwide insurrection escalates, this is the unremitting reaction of the Iranian regime's security forces. Teetering on the brink of total downfall, the theocratic regime is thrashing out in the only way it knows.... violent repression. It has had plenty of practice. Brutal coercion, arbitrary arrest, torture, and execution have been the core tools of the mullahs since they hijacked the revolution that overthrew the Shah in 1979. Women have been treated as second class citizens in a system of misogynistic, female apartheid. The brutal murder of 22-year-old Mahsa Amini by the so-called morality police, for not wearing her hijab properly, was the spark that ignited the uprising. Ironically, her arrest and murder arose following an order for the morality police to tighten up the imposition of tough dress codes on women, by the Iranian President Ebrahim Raisi – 'The Butcher of Tehran'. He may inadvertently have set in motion the revolution that will topple him and his fundamentalist cohorts from power. Led by brave women, the protests have escalated day by day and have enveloped all 31 Iranian provinces and all towns and cities. At the time of writing there have already been over 750 deaths, including 77 children and teenagers, and more than 30,000 protesters have been arrested. 4 of the young protesters have been tortured into signing false confessions, then hanged. Many others have been sentenced to death. In the past year, the mullahs' regime has executed over 550 people, in a wave of killings designed to smash opposition. Many of those sentenced have been accused of "*moharebeh*" or "waging war against God," a charge which carries the mandatory death penalty in Iran.

Figure 39 - Mahsa Amini – killed by the 'morality police' in September 2022, for not wearing her hijab properly.

JFK famously said that "Those who make peaceful revolution impossible will make violent revolution inevitable." The truth of his statement can be seen on the streets of Tehran and other Iranian towns and cities, where protesters have lost their fear; where they throw rocks and Molotov cocktails at heavily armed members of the elite IRGC and torch posters of the Supreme Leader, Ayatollah Ali Khamenei and his criminal president Ebrahim Raisi. Streets have been blocked with barricades and burning trash cans and Basij offices and vehicles have been set on fire. Already there are signs of IRGC men and their Basij paramilitary colleagues refusing to turn up for duty and even refusing to open fire on their fellow countrymen and women. The turning point in the uprising is near. The people, in particular the younger generation, have had enough. Students at 45 of Iran's leading universities have joined the insurrection. Secondary and even primary school children have boycotted classes and marched through towns and cities chanting "Death to the dictator" and "Death to Khamenei."

At long last, western media and politicians have been jolted awake by the unfolding revolution. Years of protests in Iran, that always ended in bloody reprisals by the theocratic state, were repeatedly swept under the carpet of western appeasement, as spineless political leaders and journalists tried to build a case for lifting sanctions and reviving Barack Obama's deeply flawed nuclear deal, in order to throw a lifeline to the clerical dictatorship. Escalating evidence of the torture and execution of political prisoners occasioned nothing more than infrequent, mild complaints. The shooting dead of more than 1,500 demonstrators during peaceful protests in late 2019, elicited a sharp rebuke from the UN, but no independent inquiry and no attempt to hold the perpetrators to account. Once again, western politicians clamoured to persuade the Iranian regime to sign up to a re-hashed and entirely delusional nuclear agreement, despite clear-cut evidence that the mullahs were accelerating their plans to build a nuclear weapon.

Instead of supporting the repressed people of Iran and backing their main, democratic opposition movement, the PMOI/MEK, the west tried to invent a tenuous narrative of hardliners versus reformists inside the regime, as if somehow peace, justice, freedom and democracy could be restored by replacing one set of turbaned tyrants with another. It was a dangerous fantasy. Even now, apologists for the mullahs are arguing that the rebellion is spontaneous and leaderless and therefore lacks cohesion and is doomed to fail. This is a purposefully misleading depiction of the situation. For many years, MEK Resistance Units have been established in towns and cities throughout Iran. In the past five years they have grown exponentially, backed and coordinated by their remarkable leader, Mrs Maryam Rajavi. These courageous Resistance Units have played a vital role in initiating and managing the on-going protests, as well as guiding the direction of the uprising by focusing on the core demand of the Iranian people for regime change.

Figure 40 - Women protesting in the nationwide uprising in Iran.

On Friday, October 28, 2022, the mullahs called for pro-regime demonstrations following the official Friday Prayer ceremony. This was a total failure, as people continued their protests well after midnight on the Friday. Then the IRGC Chief, Hossein Salami, warned protesters that Saturday would be their last day of taking to the streets. His statement was a clear acknowledgement of the regime's failure to quell the Iranian people's nationwide uprising. It was also an indication of the regime's intention to further intensify its brutal suppression of the protests. In particular, Khamenei's representatives have been instructed to focus their attacks on the MEK and its role in the uprising. The regime is seriously concerned about the MEK's network activities inside Iran.

Now that evidence has emerged of Iranian military advisors on the ground in Ukraine, instructing the Russians on the use of their kamikaze drones, it is clear that the mullahs have, for the first time, become involved in a major war on the European continent. They have supplied Vladimir Putin with thousands of these lethal drones, which his forces have used extensively to kill and maim innocent Ukrainian civilians and to destroy their power plants and vital infrastructure. There are reports that the Iranian regime is even supplying Russia with missiles. Surely this must be the last straw for the West. Surely the time has come to put the IRGC, MOIS, and the supreme leader's network of organizations and their affiliated entities on the terror list, close our embassies in Tehran and withdraw our ambassadors, while simultaneously expelling all Iranian diplomatic staff and their agents from western nations? The focus of the west must now be on regime change in Iran and supporting the Iranian people.

Dictatorships never survive. If you compare the Iranian dictatorship with, say the Soviet Union, you can see clear parallels. In the 1970's, the Soviet Union could have chosen to set aside their ideological communist philosophy and instead, sought to improve the economy and improve the welfare of their people. They chose to stick rigidly to their ideology and in doing so, sowed the seeds of their own ultimate demise. The Islamic Republic of Iran has reached a similar fork in the road, and they also are incapable of abandoning their warped fundamentalist ideology. For if they do embark on any kind of reform, they will face internal disintegration, and if they don't, they will face the overthrow of their regime at the hands of the Iranian people, and this is the quandary that they cannot resolve. They too will implode internally as a result and there are already signs of that happening.

The mullahs have also positioned themselves strategically in the Middle East as pro-Palestine, anti-Israel, anti-American, in an effort to recruit allies in a predominantly Sunni-Arab environment. They know that simply waving a Persian Shi'ite flag would not attract the support they require. But their strategy has been unwound by their outright backing for Bashar al-Assad's bloody civil war in Syria, where he has wantonly murdered hundreds of thousands of Sunni-Arabs. Similarly, the Iranian regime's support for Hezbollah in Lebanon, the Houthi rebels in Yemen and the Shi'ite militias in Iraq is deeply unpopular in Iran, where the population are enraged at the vast resources being used to facilitate these regional proxy-wars, while they face economic penury at home.

Their seemingly pro-Palestine policy too has been severely detrimental, not only to the Iranian nation, but to the Palestinian people as well, as it has propped up fundamentalist-Islamic groups as impediments to the formation of a united and independent Palestinian government, causing awkward fraying of the Palestinian political domain.

Iran has one of the highest rates of brain-drain in the world, with most of its highly intelligent and entrepreneurial elite fleeing abroad, desperate to escape the constant repression and aggressive fundamentalism. Even the children and grandchildren of the first-generation revolutionaries like Khamenei, are commonly to be found partying and enjoying the high life in Dubai and Europe.

The revolutionary zeal is gradually dissipating. The tipping point has been reached. But if you compare Iran today with the last days of the Shah, you can see that the mullahs and their IRGC protectors have their backs against the wall. During the reign of the Shah, most of the ruling elite had been educated abroad, had purchased properties abroad, spoke foreign languages and had friends and business associates outside of Iran. They had places to run to if they lost power. The mullahs and the IRGC elite have none of these attributes. Most of the mullahs were educated in seminaries in Qom, or for the revolutionary guards, their main educational experience was military training during the Iran-Iraq war. The regime is virtually friendless. Apart from Bashar al-Assad's Syria, they have nowhere to run to if things go wrong and few would wish to spend their retirement in Syria. They have no plan B, and they are willing to kill systematically to cling to power. Although there is only a tiny proportion of the 80 million population who retain control, they routinely execute or imprison anyone who could threaten their authority. It will take another revolution to oust them.

It is madness for Western appeasers to maintain dialogue with Iran in this catastrophic adventure. Instead of aiding and abetting the Iranian mullahs the West should be standing shoulder to shoulder with the beleaguered Iranian people who want an end to the theocratic fascist regime that has tortured, executed, and oppressed them for over four decades under its perverted version of Islam.

But Khamenei and the regime have played a devious cat and mouse game with the West. Tehran is desperate to have sanctions lifted to aid its crippled economy and it is a past master at duping the West. The theocratic regime knows that appeasing Iran has been the benchmark of Western Middle East policy for years. The West literally allows Iran to get away with murder. That's why, during the talks in Vienna, scant mention has been made of Iran's appalling human rights record, where it now executes more people than any other country in the world apart from China and while its fundamentalist rulers pour billions into brutal foreign wars.

Khamenei and his regime are at a deadly impasse and cannot resolve increasing crises at home and abroad. Neither Ebrahim Raisi nor a potential nuclear weapon can save the mullahs because the restive population does not accept the regime. Khamenei's strategy of using Raisi as the bogyman has miserably backfired as the insurrection in Iran gets ever closer to achieving its goal, regime change for freedom and democracy. Raisi's policy has been a disaster on the economic front as mismanagement, incompetence and corruption have led to a tanking economy and a catastrophic environmental crisis, including water shortages, floods, and other calamities.

Chapter Twenty-Three

A BRIGHT FUTURE BECKONS

Albania is becoming a popular destination for senior political figures from America. In May 2022, Mike Pompeo, the 70th US Secretary of State, travelled to Albania to visit Ashraf 3, the PMOI/MEK headquarters. The former Secretary of State's trip to the MEK compound in Albania was followed on 23rd June 2022 by a momentous visit by Mike Pence, the 48th US Vice President. The former Vice President and his wife Karen were welcomed by Mrs Maryam Rajavi, president-elect of the NCRI. His bombshell visit came as a body-blow to the theocratic and fundamentalist fascist regime who have oppressed Iran's 80 million population for more than four decades.

Addressing the 3,000 MEK resistance leaders in Ashraf-3, Mike Pence said: "It's a privilege for us to be here in the home of thousands of courageous Iranian men and women. A home of peace and prosperity. A home of hope for a free and democratic Iran. You know I've travelled more than 5,000 miles from my home in Indiana to be here today because we share one common cause: the liberation of the Iranian people from decades of tyranny and the rebirth of a free, peaceful, prosperous, and democratic Iran." Turning his attention to the president of the Islamic Republic – Ebrahim Raisi - the former Vice President continued: "Ebrahim Raisi is unworthy of leading the great people of Iran. He must be removed from office by the people of Iran, and he must be prosecuted for the crimes against humanity and genocide that he perpetrated 30 years ago and every day since."

Mike Pence continued: "The resistance movement in Iran has never been stronger. It's been inspiring for me to learn today even more resistance units in Iran are the centre of hope for the Iranian people, an engine for change from within during the uprisings and continued protests. And every day it's clear they're growing stronger while the regime grows weaker." Echoing similar sentiments expressed by Mike Pompeo during his visit to Ashraf-3, Mike Pence said: "A renewed Iran nuclear deal won't benefit the people of Iran in any way. It will merely empower and enrich a corrupt regime that has tormented and tortured the Iranian people for generations. Today, we call on the Biden administration to immediately withdraw from all nuclear negotiations with Tehran, voice support for the organized opposition in Iran, and make it clear that America and our allies will never permit the regime in Tehran to obtain a nuclear weapon."

Figure 41 - Former US Vice President Mike Pence

Responding to the address, Mrs Maryam Rajavi said: "The MEK was the first to expose the regime's nuclear projects since 1991. In 2002, it uncovered the regime's secret sites and informed the world of its bomb-making program. Without those revelations, the mullahs would have obtained the bomb years ago. The world is witnessing that conditions are ripe for change in Iran and that people are ready for change. Protests are erupting with increasing intensity across the country. On the other hand, the regime has no answer except stepping up repression, executions, or torture in its prisons. The people of Iran have the right to resist, much like the war of independence in America. The mullahs have occupied our country. People now chant, "Our enemy is right here; they lie when they say it's America."

Criticizing appeasers in the West, Mrs Rajavi continued: "Today, the world clearly sees that the policy of appeasement of the mullahs has failed. This is a regime that gives a bomb to its diplomat to blow up the gathering of the Iranian resistance where hundreds of distinguished international personalities were present."

Mike Pence assured his MEK audience in Ashraf-3 that Mrs Rajavi's 10-point plan for a free and democratic Iran is the only way forward for that country's beleaguered citizens. The plan calls for the formation of a republic based on the separation of religion from the state, pluralism, and the stated freedoms in the Universal Declaration of Human Rights. The 10-point plan has been welcomed by ordinary Iranians and enjoys the support of a wide range of parliaments and prominent personalities in Europe and the United States.

He also importantly pointed out: "Your Resistance Units' commitment to democracy, human rights, and freedom for every citizen is a vision for a free Iran and an inspiration to the world. Maryam Rajavi's Ten Point Plan for the future of Iran will ensure the freedom of expression, the freedom of assembly, and freedom for every Iranian to choose their elected leaders. It's a foundation on which to build the future of a free Iran. The regime in Tehran wants to trick the world into believing that the Iranian protesters want to return to the dictatorship of the Shah as well. But I want to assure you, we're not confused by their lies."

The former Vice President concluded: "Let me thank Maryam Rajavi and all of those gathered here at Ashraf 3 for offering hope to your people in Iran. Your Resistance Units, commitment to democracy, human rights and freedom for every citizen is a vision for a free Iran and an inspiration to the world. Maryam Rajavi's Ten-Point Plan for the future of Iran will ensure the freedom of expression, the freedom of assembly, freedom for every Iranian to choose their elected leaders. It's a foundation on which to build the future of a free Iran."

An Iran without the mullahs has the distinct advantage of already having a parliament and president-in-exile, that are ready, willing, and able, to stabilize Iran for the six-month period between the fall of the mullahs and the free and fair democratic elections that will allow the people to elect their leaders. The parliament is the National Council of Resistance of Iran and its President-elect is Maryam Rajavi. This means there's no danger of Iran falling under the power of a sectarian group or requiring outside help to establish a democracy. It also means that the Iranian people and the world know what to expect from a free Iran under Maryam Rajavi. The ten-point plan referred to by Mike Pence offers a bright future for a free and democratic Iran, following the overthrow of the clerical dictatorship.

The Ten Point Plan

1. Rejection of velayat-e faqih (absolute clerical rule). Affirmation of the people's sovereignty in a republic founded on universal suffrage and pluralism.
2. Freedom of speech, freedom of political parties, freedom of assembly, freedom of the press and the internet. Dissolution and disbanding of the Islamic Revolutionary Guard Corps (IRGC), the terrorist Qods Force, plainclothes groups, the unpopular Basij, the Ministry of Intelligence, Council of the Cultural Revolution, and all suppressive patrols and institutions in cities, villages, schools, universities, offices, and factories.
3. Commitment to individual and social freedoms and rights in accordance with the Universal Declaration of Human Rights. Disbanding all agencies in charge of censorship and inquisition.

Seeking justice for massacred political prisoners, prohibition of torture, and the abolition of the death penalty.

4. Separation of religion and state,[93] and freedom of religions and faiths.
5. Complete gender equality in the realms of political, social, cultural, and economic rights, and equal participation of women in political leadership. Abolition of any form of discrimination; the right to choose one's own clothing freely; the right to freely marry and divorce, and to obtain education and employment. Prohibition of all forms of exploitation against women under any pretext.
6. An independent judiciary and legal system consistent with international standards based on the presumption of innocence, the right to defense counsel, right of appeal, and the right to be tried in a public court. Full independence of judges. Abolition of the mullahs' Sharia law and dissolution of Islamic Revolutionary Courts.
7. Autonomy for and removal of double injustices against Iranian nationalities and ethnicities consistent with the NCRI's plan for the autonomy of Iranian Kurdistan;
8. Justice and equal opportunities in the realms of employment and entrepreneurship for all people of Iran in a free market economy. Restoration of the rights of blue-collar workers, farmers, nurses, white-collar workers, teachers, and retirees.
9. Protection and rehabilitation of the environment, which has been decimated under the rule of the mullahs.
10. A non-nuclear Iran[94] that is also devoid of weapons of mass destruction. Peace, co-existence, and international and regional cooperation.

John Lennon wrote his famous song "Imagine", inviting us to consider a perfect world. Perfection may be difficult to achieve, but for the 80 million suffering and oppressed people of Iran, imagining

---

[93] Rajavi, Maryam. 2016. For secularism in Iran. https://www.maryam-rajavi.com/en/viewpoints/for-secularism-in-iran/.

[94] Rajavi, Maryam. 2021. "The regime's nuclear program." https://www.maryam-rajavi.com/en/viewpoints/regime-program-nuclear-free-iran/.

a better future, without the mullahs, may be the first necessary step on the way to achieving it.

Iran is facing social collapse, enduring the triple whammy of a corrupt, theocratic dictatorship, a disintegrating economy, and a manifestly bungled attempt to control the coronavirus pandemic. The mullahs' regime lost control of the economy and lost control of the disease. Having stolen the people's wealth for more than four decades since the 1979 revolution, squandering billions on the export of terror and on proxy wars, spending billions more on their top-secret nuclear weapons program, while stuffing bags of cash into their own private bank accounts, they are now facing economic and social meltdown.

The Iranian people have long known that the regime is more toxic than the covid virus. The mullahs are terrified that their theocratic system will come tumbling down, as the impoverished masses have risen up in fury and will throw them into the dustbin of history. Iran's descent into economic chaos can be laid directly at the door of supreme leader Ali Khamenei. Their policy of aggressive military expansionism and conflict across the Middle East has seen them consistently pour resources into Bashar al-Assad's murderous civil war in Syria, the genocidal campaign against the Sunni population of neighbouring Iraq, their support for the Houthi rebels in Yemen and their vast funding for the Hezbollah terrorists in Lebanon and Hamas in Gaza. They pay $750 million every year to Hezbollah in Lebanon alone. This is clearly no longer sustainable.

The people of Iran need to imagine what life would be like without the mullahs. With a democratically elected government restoring freedom, justice, human rights, and women's rights, ending the sponsorship of terror and proxy wars, ending the race to build a nuclear weapon and ending corruption, the economy of Iran would be transformed. Although the coronavirus lockdown affected the world in an unprecedented way and it will certainly take years to recover, Iran's recovery could be dynamic by comparison. Iran has the world's second-largest gas reserves and fourth-largest crude oil reserves. The combination of sanctions and the collapse in oil prices due to the pandemic has brought Iran's greatest industry to a shuddering halt. But with the lockdown over, people around the world have rushed back into cars and aircraft and oil and gas prices have risen again. Iran would be in a prime position to benefit from this resurgence, but only if the mullahs have been deposed, democracy restored, and sanctions lifted.

Figure 42 - PMOI/MEK supporters in the West call for Iran freedom

The Iranian people also have to imagine what life would be like if they had a new government that no longer spent billions every year on internal oppression and the development of nuclear weapons and accompanying missile technology. Imagine the billions that is channelled to Syria, Yemen, Iraq, Lebanon, and Gaza being spent instead on schools, hospitals and social welfare in Iran. Imagine the money that has been corruptly stolen from the Iranian people by Khamenei and the IRGC being restored to its rightful owners, the people of Iran. Imagine the billions in international assets that have been frozen by sanctions, being freed for use in rebuilding the Iranian economy. The active Iranian work force is 26 million, of whom at least 10 million were jobless even before COVID-19 struck. Youth unemployment was at a staggering 40 percent. At least 70 percent of the population are living at or under the absolute poverty line, unable to meet their essential daily needs.

These are life-or-death choices for the Iranian people. They are fed up with their corrupt, fundamentalist rulers. They are fed up with living in poverty and deprivation, as the mullahs siphon off the country's wealth to fill their coffers and to finance conflict and terror throughout the Middle East. They know that the regime's system of velayat-e-faqih, the guardianship of the Islamic jurist, offers no solution to the economic crisis and no future for Iran. The whole Iranian economy is focused on the military requirements of the IRGC. Iranian society is facing chaos and social collapse. The capacity of the regime to reform the economy is no longer there. Instead, the mullahs turn their attention to test firing new missiles and demonizing the main democratic opposition movement, the PMOI/MEK to hide the reality of their economic mismanagement and to survive their inevitable fate, being overthrown at the hands of the people. The time for change has arrived. A bright future beckons for Iran.

STRUAN STEVENSON

Struan Stevenson is the Coordinator of the Campaign for Iran Change (CiC). He was a member of the European Parliament representing Scotland (1999-2014), president of the Parliament's Delegation for Relations with Iraq (2009-14) and chairman of the Friends of a Free Iran Intergroup (2004-14). Struan is also Chair of the 'In Search of Justice' (ISJ) committee on the protection of political freedoms in Iran. He is an international lecturer and is also president of the European Iraqi Freedom Association (EIFA).

Figure 43 - Struan Stevenson

CPSIA information can be obtained
at www.ICGtesting.com
Printed in the USA
BVHW061257240323
661082BV00021B/745